ETHICS: THE DRAMA OF THE MORAL LIFE

ETHICS
The Drama of the Moral Life

Piotr Jaroszynski and Mathew Anderson

ST PAULS

Alba
House

Originally published in Polish under the title: Etyka: Dramat zycia moralnego
Translated by Hugh McDonald

Library of Congress Cataloging-in-Publication Data

Jaroszynski, Piotr.
  [Etyka. English]
  Ethics : the drama of the moral life / Piotr Jaroszynski & Mathew
Anderson ; [translated by Hugh McDonald].
      p. cm.
  Includes bibliographical references.
  ISBN 0-8189-0956-0
  1. Christian ethics—Catholic authors. I. Anderson, Mathew. II.
Title.
  BJ1249.J3713 2003
  170—dc21
                        2003008188

Produced and designed in the United States of America by the
Fathers and Brothers of the Society of St. Paul,
2187 Victory Boulevard, Staten Island, New York 10314-6603,
as part of their communications apostolate.

ISBN: 0-8189-0956-0

Printing Information:

Current Printing - first digit   1   2   3   4   5   6   7   8   9   10

Year of Current Printing - first year shown

2003   2004   2005   2006   2007   2008   2009   2010   2011   2012

To our beloved Holy Father,
John Paul II,
asking for his blessing and that he may
graciously receive this work concerning the
understanding of human morality.

Table of Contents

Castel Gandolfo, 20 września 1997 r.

+   Drogi Panie Profesorze,

Po zapoznaniu się z ofiarowaną mi książką
"Etyka, dramat życia moralnego", pragnę serdecznie
podziękować Autorowi również za Jego dedykację
dla mnie. Bóg zapłać!

Niech Boże błogosławieństwo towarzyszy Panu
Profesorowi w Jego pracy naukowej i dydaktycznej.
Szczęść Boże!

Jan Paweł II

Pan
Prof.dr hab.Piotr Jaroszyński
KUL
Al.Racławickie 14
20-950 Lublin

Translation of the letter from His Holiness John Paul II
to Professor Jaroszynski:

Castel Gandolfo, September 20, 1997

Dear Professor,

After acquainting myself with the book *Ethics: The Drama of the Moral Life* which was given to me, I would like to thank the author from my heart as well for his dedication to me. May God reward him!

May God's blessing accompany Professor Jaroszynski in his scientific and didactic work.

May God bless!

John Paul II

Acknowledgments

I am grateful to the many people who played a role in this project in so many different ways. It would be impossible to acknowledge them all here, but I especially want to recognize the following:

Sarah Anderson

Wojciech Antczak

Anna, Grzegorz Jaroszynscy

Irena Jellaczyc - Habrowska

Alina, Ludwik Makowieccy

Krystyna, Adam Kurzaj

Frank Lennox

Stanislawa Malyszko

Hugh McDonald

Father Paul McDonald

Marek Michalski

Janina, Bogdan Michalowscy

Jerzy Sliwinski

Barbara Wieczorek

Iwona, Leon Zawadowscy

Heartfelt thanks!
Piotr Jaroszynski

Preface to the English Edition

A reflective person will already know the great need for a moral compass in our society today. Yet, morality has become a taboo topic in our public and social discourse. Moral precepts are either dismissed as religious dogma or they are treated lightly, even ridiculed in popular culture. In this milieu, how does one learn about and live out a moral life? This book, *Ethics: The Drama of the Moral Life*, presents the essentials for living a good life. Morality is anything but a dry and rigid set of rules. The moral life is in fact an active drama that engages the noblest faculties of the person. A soldier who faces an enemy, a teenager who resists the temptation to drugs or pre-marital sex or a business person who is honest in his dealings is hardly living a boring life. Far from being detached or aloof from the so-called real world, each of these people is actively engaging in the complex and dynamic journey which is the moral life.

At the heart of this drama is the decision. Since human beings have an intellect and a will, that is the ability to reason and the freedom to choose, the moment of decision lies at the heart of all morality. *Ethics: The Drama of the Moral Life* presents the simple but timeless maxim that a decision which is in agreement with one's conscience is morally good while one that goes against the conscience is morally evil. However, the conscience is not an infallible God-like guide, but a faculty that is shaped and molded throughout life. In our modern technological society with its mass-media-driven culture, the conscience is much more susceptible to a greater number of influences and consequently has a greater need for vigilant protection and nurturing.

In its presentation of ethics this book avoids two extremes: relativism and absolutism. The former reduces everything to personal subjectivity or individual circumstances, while the latter reduces everything to duty or to a list of objective rules that are to be scrupulously followed. To the contrary, this book sees the grandeur of the moral life as being rooted within the subjective person who finds his actualization through the objective order as understood by reason. The objective order is not something that is imposed on us arbitrarily by some external power, rather it is that which perfects us and helps us reach our potential as human persons. While in fact there are norms that are binding on all persons, the moral good consists not so much in adherence to a rule or bringing our external actions into conformity with a certain code as much as it lies in the harmony between our own inner inclinations and decisions with the objective good — that which perfects us. This is where the virtues come in because virtues help us more easily recognize, choose and move toward what is objectively good and beneficial to us and to the society in which we live. *Ethics: The Drama of the Moral Life* highlights the role of virtues or good habits and inclinations in the moral life.

This presentation of ethics is in keeping with the approach taken by many classical philosophers. One such philosopher, Josef Pieper, argued in *The Four Cardinal Virtues*[1] that a presentation

---

[1] Pieper, Josef. *The Four Cardinal Virtues*, pp. 11-12.

of ethics which focuses on commandments and obligations runs the risk of creating arbitrary lists and tends to forget the human person in the process. On the other hand an ethics of virtue is free from unnecessary regimentation and restriction while remaining cognizant of universal maxims. A virtue-based ethics centers around the common makeup of the human person along with individual differences so that each person can become what he ought to become — prudent, just, brave and temperate.

With this paradigm in mind, this book introduces the basic notions of ethics to the reader. It is not an attempt to offer solutions to the moral problems of the day or to explain all the concepts that are relevant to specialized fields of ethics such as business or medicine. Rather, the purpose of this book is to help the reader develop an understanding of and appreciation for the timeless principles of classical ethics which can and do serve as a moral compass in any age. Hopefully, this book will provide the reader with a context and foundation from which to make judgments about the ethical issues of our times and most especially the ethical situations that confront us in our own daily lives.

It is important to note that this book presents a philosophy of ethics, not a moral theology; that is, it relies upon the trustworthiness of reason for its foundation, and not on religious belief or divine faith. While both of the authors are practicing Christians and have a great respect for Divine revelation, they also recognize the need in our pluralistic society for a presentation of basic moral principles that can be grasped without resorting to a particular religious faith. The heroic manner in which Socrates faced death points to our natural ability to grasp the natural moral law and is an inspiration to those seeking to live a virtuous and reasonably happy life. Furthermore, an understanding of the natu-

ral virtues is germane and important to every society, whether secu-
lar or religious, including Christian societies.

The study of ethics is generally preceded by the study of other
philosophical disciplines such as epistemology (how we know
things) and metaphysics (the nature of being). Unlike most other
ethics texts, this book explains some of the ideas from these fields
which are germane to the understanding of the subject matter at
hand; for example, in order to understand what perfects a human
being, it is necessary to have some idea of the nature of human
beings. To assist the student reader, we have study / reflection
questions and supplemental readings at the end of each section of
the text. Additionally, there is a lexicon of philosophical terms and
an extensive reading list at the end of the book. The purpose of
the lexicon is to give the reader a working definition of terms with
which they may be unfamiliar; it is not intended to be an exhaus-
tive or definitive explanation of terms. The questions at the end
of each section are designed to help the reader review and apply
the concepts presented in that section. Those who wish to deepen
and broaden their understanding of key concepts beyond the contents of this introductory book may wish to consult the supplemental readings cited at the end of each section and at the end of
the book.

In closing, I would like to say a little about how this book
came into being. Dr. Piotr Jaroszynski, the primary author, originally wrote this book as an ethics text for high school students in
Poland. This work was part of the important task of reintroduc-
ing to the Polish academic milieu those gems of Western and
Christian civilization that had become lost to it under the cen-
sorship of communism. It has been a great privilege and honor to
collaborate with Dr. Jaroszynski in adapting this book for its cur-

rent audience. Dr. Jaroszynski and I have written the English edition not only for the student who will use this as a textbook in an ethics class, but also for those individuals who do not have a teacher to guide them through this course. The independent reader will find the lexicon, study questions and supplemental readings useful aids to their learning.

As one can see from the acknowledgments section, many people played a role in bringing this project to fruition. Hugh McDonald's excellent translation as well as his insights into both the Polish and North American cultures were invaluable to this book. Although he was not connected directly with this project, I wish to thank Robert Sweetman of the Institute for Christian Studies for his patient guidance of my philosophical studies and for giving me new insights into aspects of classical philosophy. A special thanks to Avery Cardinal Dulles, SJ, Dr. Vittorio Possenti from the University of Venice and Dr. Donald DeMarco from Saint Jerome's University for taking the time and interest to review the manuscript, provide suggestions and offer their encouraging endorsements of this book. Most importantly, my sincere and heartfelt thanks goes to my wife Sarah Anderson who spent innumerable hours assisting and supporting me in this project. Last but not least, my thanks to our publisher, Alba House, for expertly seeing to the myriad of details that go into transforming a manuscript into the volume currently in the reader's hands.

Mathew Anderson

Foreword to the Polish Edition

Our moral health is no less important than our biological health. Perhaps it is more important, since even under today's circumstances it is necessary for the survival and growth of the nation. Our Polish nation has been weakened more over the last fifty years by the Nazi and Soviet occupations than during the three centuries when it was divided between Prussia, Russia and Austria. Our nation's health is threatened from many directions. From without, we see environmental pollution, the poisoning of the land, the forests, water and air, and the exploitation of our natural resources carried out in a deliberately destructive manner. Internally, we have seen a propaganda of deception in all sections of our culture. We have seen the introduction of the so-called socialist morality based on deception and class hatred. We have seen how the elements of religion and Christian morality have been cast out of the schools and from our publications. We can see the results, and the effects still pose a threat to us as individuals and as a society.

While the damage done to the environment and the economy can be repaired by technology and economic reforms, the moral damage to society is more difficult to repair, and it cannot be done quickly. We need a deeper understanding of morality and a great moral effort. It is easy to destroy the moral order and good customs, but it is very difficult to rebuild them once they are gone. This reconstruction requires that we master once again the difficult knowledge of ethics, especially with regard to social and moral vices such as the lack of respect for others' property, drunkenness, drug abuse, divorce, the mass killing of those who are defenseless, even the unborn. The first task is to free ourselves from the false and widespread opinions that are the fruit of decades of indoctrination. We must meditate deeply upon the lasting principles of ethics. These principles arose from the experience and practice of all men over many ages. They were formulated in ancient times, as far back as our historical memory and religious traditions can reach.

When Poland became a nation over a thousand years ago, we received the universal human morality together with the Christian religion. The theory of human moral conduct was constructed by the thinkers of ancient Greece and Rome, and refined by the thinkers of Christian Europe, especially Saint Thomas Aquinas. It rests upon solid philosophical principles. This theory has become what we call classical ethics. It has roots both in biblical culture and the philosophical thought of the ancient world. It is this theory of moral conduct that is presented in this book. Piotr Jaroszynski, a professor of philosophy at the Catholic University of Lublin, has written a very good presentation of classical ethics. It is accessible to the average reader. It is well thought out, clear and concise. The author wanted to be part of the living and powerful movement of classical philosophy, and to present the known and recognized formulations and well-grounded solutions to moral problems, and in this he has succeeded well. He has shown the human character of the drama of action that finds its focal point in acts of personal decision motivated by the concrete good of man. Man is perfected in his rationality by the virtues, which "firmly, promptly, and with pleasure" (*firmiter, prompte, delectabiliter*) enable us to realize our highest human potentialities. The virtues, although they are neglected in casuistic and merely deontological ethics, "make the man himself good, and make his deeds noble."

It is good that this book was formulated as it was, that it will contribute to the return of ethics in our schools, that it will reintroduce the ethical principles that have withstood the test of the centuries. It will help our youth to discover the rational character of the Good.

Father Mieczyslaw Albert Krapiec

Introduction

Classical ethics is one of the crown jewels of Western civilization. I have written this book in an attempt to reacquaint today's readers with the beauty of this jewel. Although some branches of learning have a long history, our memory of things past may be obscured by our amazement at the latest achievements. Some sciences, such as mathematics, incorporate the discoveries of the past and continue to make progress. There are other forgotten disciplines, such as alchemy and astrology, which are no longer treated as sciences. However, there are still others that have successfully stood the test of time and to which we are constantly returning. Among these sciences, classical ethics has the first place.

Today, we are fascinated by progress, and so we find it hard to accept the idea that ancient societies may have known something which we do not know today. We are even more surprised when we discover that this forgotten knowledge is not some carefully guarded mystery, but a simple matter that concerns everyone. Morality is permanently and essentially inscribed into human life. Each person is the author of his own decisions, and these decisions are either good or evil. It does not matter whether the person is an American, a Pole, a Frenchman or a German. It does not matter whether he lives today, or lived in ancient Greece or Rome, or in medieval Europe. Each of us is or was responsible for his decisions. Each person constantly faces moments of decision. Even to refuse to make a decision is a decision, and so it is

either a good decision or a bad one. We cannot escape from decisions or morality. However, the decline of classical education has
the result that we are often lost when we try to understand morality. It is true that each person has some degree of common sense
and that each person has a conscience, but we are subject to the
pressures of different ideologies and customs. When we make a
decision, we are also influenced by various philosophies and the
physical sciences. The result is that the good we choose is often a
good in appearance only, and that we become indifferent to evil.
The result of the decline in moral knowledge is the impoverish-
ment of our moral lives and our degradation as human persons.

When we know the foundations of ethics, our intellectual
horizons are broadened, and we become more sensitive to moral
issues. We have inherited the foundations of ethics from many
great philosophers, such as Plato, Aristotle, Saint Augustine and
Saint Thomas Aquinas. These authors are pillars of Western culture.

Over the past century we have had the bitter experience of
the dangers that come from ideology. In the name of false values
packaged in noble slogans, hundreds of millions of people have
been murdered or have had their rights violated. The mass media
have also served us with examples of false freedom. People have
lost the ability to take a stand on their own. They have been taught
to overlook evil and to lose themselves in pleasure. Some modern
philosophers have created the ideal of a man who is beyond good
and evil, while other philosophers present us with unattainable
ideals and values. Many psychologists, sociologists and other scientists present a picture of man in which human freedom has dis-
appeared, where human activity seems to be determined entirely
by biological, psychological and cultural factors. When we do not

have a strong cultural heritage to counteract the above influences and provide support and moral guidance, we find ourselves lost and helpless. Many people find guidance in their religion and try to appeal to their religious beliefs to support their ethics, but there are many religions and not everyone has a religion. No matter what his individual situation, each person is still forced by life itself to make decisions, often difficult ones. What then?

Classical ethics provides a way to deal with these problems. It shows the rational foundations of human action, why some actions are good and others are evil, and the proper value of morality in human life. Western culture is unique in that it was the first culture to recognize properly the sovereignty of the human person. Man is a subject and person, and for this reason he must always be treated as an end, and never as a mere means in our action. Man as a person is not a mere part of nature in the strict sense, nor is he a mere part of society or the state. Even though as a member of a society or a citizen in a state he has many ties that bind him to others, a man is something higher than the state and higher than society. The state and other societies are relational beings rather than substances. Society is not something that exists in and of itself; its existence is rooted in people who are subjects or substances. (Classical philosophers use the term "substance" to describe real beings; other ways of existing, such as relations, are called "accidents".) In other cultures, man was constantly reduced to being a mere part of a greater whole with no value as an individual. Ethics, often formed and strengthened by religion, would lose sight of an authentic concern for man. However, if man as a person is the end or purpose of action, then moral or religious rules or laws that do not reckon with this are not real laws and do not create any obligation for man.

Classical ethics has often been misunderstood, especially in the areas of areteology which is the theory of the virtues, and the connection between classical ethics and the Christian religion. Christianity assimilated Greek and Roman culture, and the result is that today people treat many moral questions as belonging exclusively to religion and faith. As a result, they think that whether one moral position is better than another is merely a question of faith. If this is so, then they accept moral principles as binding for members of their religious community, but not for society as a whole. The result is a dangerous indifference to moral principles at the social level. Christian philosophers, especially Saint Thomas Aquinas, however, make a clear distinction between the order of faith and the order of natural knowledge or reason. Faith and reason come together into a whole that is known as Christian culture, but we must be clear that faith and reason are distinct from each other. Faith is largely a matter of the will and grace while reason is a matter of the intellect. A large part of Christian ethics comes not only from faith but from reason as well, and the proof of this is that the pre-Christian Greeks and Romans both knew this system of ethics before Christianity. Today, however, because many have little knowledge of history, philosophy, theology and ethics, they tend to lump faith and knowledge together. Despite this tendency in our time, an educated person should know how to make the proper distinctions between things. Morality places an obligation upon each person, whether or not he has religious faith. Classical ethics teaches us about this universally obligatory morality.

We should not be afraid that the theory of virtues would mechanize man's moral life. Virtues are moral skills and habits. Just as we must develop skills in art, science, and other parts of our lives, we must also develop moral skills. The philosophical theory of virtues is not intended to make us into trained animals. A trained animal does what we want, but an educated man with a solid ethical formation knows best how to do what he wants. The moral virtues such as prudence and justice make it easier for us to recognize and pursue what is truly good. Since the moral life is about personal decisions and concrete goods, there is no formula that can be applied to every situation. This is why the virtues, which are skills or habits rather than formulas or mechanical rules, are so important.

1

Good and End: The Object of Human Acts

We associate good and evil with morality, but they are not limited to the field of morality. Good and evil play some role in all of man's acts, but we can also speak of good and evil in nature and the whole universe. We speak of education, art, religion, a car, a house, the sun, stars, and the earth with all its riches as good things. We want to define more precisely the field of moral good and evil, and we must first take a closer look at the good as it appears in the context of human life.

When we analyze the things we do, we are struck by the fact that all these activities are done for some intended purpose. Even in a great crowd in the street or market place, each individual person is doing something. An individual might be selling or buying, calling out to someone, walking, or running. In each case he acts because he wants something and knows what he wants. That is why he walks in one direction rather than another, why he puts one item aside and looks carefully at another. Even the person who appears to be walking aimlessly is also walking with a certain purpose. Perhaps he is wandering for exercise or relaxation, or learning his way around a new neighborhood. Purpose is inscribed into all of human life. If someone gives up one purpose, another purpose appears, and another one after that.

We conclude that all our actions are called forth by some end. The end appears attractive enough to draw us to it. What power does an end possess? It is the power of the good. The good and the end or purpose are really one and the same. An end attracts us because it appears to be good, and as something good it is an end. When we are hungry, food attracts us as an end and good. When we feel like listening to music, we go to a concert as an end and good. When we are prepared to risk our life, it is because we see our country as an end and good. Human acts are always called into existence by some end and good.

We see that what we call the good cannot be limited to some single thing. There are many goods and they differ from one another. A stroll, a concert and food are all goods, but they are three very different things. In order to take action toward some end, we must first know this end, and then we must freely choose the end. Each of us knows that nothing can force us to want something. Something might exert great pressure on us, whether this is a threat, or the hope of gain and pleasure, but it is entirely up to us whether we allow ourselves to be swayed by these factors. If such pressures do influence us, we will always have in view some good, whether it is preserving our life, avoiding pain, or maintaining our professional standing. Indeed, we can resist any such influence, because we always have the option of saying no.

If the good and the end is what motivates all action, then evil can never be a motive. At first, the facts may seem to contradict this. We see so many evils in the world: war, robbery, theft, betrayal and deception. We do not need any proof to see that people are to blame for these things. Evil cannot be banished from human life. Yet this does not disprove what we are saying. Evil cannot be the primary motive for acting. It is easy to illustrate this with examples. If a thief steals, it is not for the sake of the theft, but because theft brings him something that is good, whether it is money or a work of art. A nation may wage war against another causing great devastation, but the war is not declared for the sake of mere destruction but for the sake of some good, such as the protection of freedom. If we say that theft and war are evil things, it is not because of the purpose of these actions, but because of the way the purpose is obtained.

Why can evil never be the end of action? Evil is not something in a positive sense, but only the lack of something good that should be present. The way we speak about this in everyday language can mislead us, because we speak of evil as if it were really something, whereas it is not. In order to understand evil, we must avoid this way of speaking. Some examples will help to illustrate this. A bad bridge is a bridge with gaps in it. What is bad in this bridge? That which it should have, but which is not there. If the gaps are filled, then the bridge will be good. An illness is evil. What is illness, except the lack of proper harmony in the body? When that harmony is restored, health is restored. Theft is evil, not because money is evil, but because the thief lacks the proper respect for the other person's right to his own property. Evil always appears as the lack of something, and so it is non-being in a certain respect, because if something is lacking, this means that the thing in question does not exist. In our ordinary way of speaking, we use one term to describe a thing that has certain things lacking, and the term includes both what is good and what is evil, so we ordinarily speak of the whole as evil. Plato made this error, because he treated the content of words as if they were actual objects, but he did not pay proper attention to the difference between the way things exist and the way we think about them. This led him to create his theory of ideas and also to treat evil as a positive thing. In fact, there is no such thing as evil in itself, or pure evil. Evil, as a lack or absence, is always a lack in a certain thing, in some actual object whose existence is already good. A thief is evil, but only as a thief, not as a man.

Evil, which is a lack of something and a non-being in its own right, cannot be the purpose or motive of action. If something moves us to act, it is something rather than nothing. That which moves us is something definite, such as real money, real land, real health. Each of these is a certain good. Evil may appear while we are trying to obtain a good. The thief wants money and he steals. The hungry man eats too much and becomes ill. Neither the theft nor the illness are the motive behind the activity. Even the person who commits suicide only wants relief from his suffering.

Why is it so important to present the good as the motive and purpose of activity? We may be influenced by ordinary language or by certain philosophical theories that go back as far as the Pythagoreans and Plato to think that evil is something real and that evil desires are desires which are aimed at evil things. We might believe that in each man there is one part of his being that is evil, and that when the evil part is dominant then the man becomes evil. This view of evil can lead societies to take extreme measures. If this is true, then the evil man must either be destroyed or enslaved. People will be divided beforehand into good and evil people, and things will likewise be divided into good and evil things. This leads to a totalitarian state that is ruled by harsh laws and which relies on police and military forces. Anyone who resists this kind of state is either killed or incarcerated.

There may also be more subtle consequences to the belief that evil is a real and positive thing. A man who believes that there is something in him that is evil by nature, and therefore beyond his control, will regard all action as futile and rely on Providence alone. Such a man may give up positive moral action and find refuge in a passive attitude to life, seeking consolation in religion or art.

Communist ideology is an example of a way of thinking that saw evil as an embodied reality. The communists regarded capitalism, religion, capitalists and religious believers as evil, and tried to eliminate them. On the other hand, European culture is greatly influenced today by Gnosticism and certain types of Protestantism, both of which deny that man has any power to make himself better. Man's situation, then, would be entirely under the control of supernatural powers, and the best that man could do would be to increase his self-knowledge. Morality would then concern customs and laws, but it would not have anything to do with man's inner self. In this picture, the drama of the moral life would disappear, leaving only cold calculation. Does it pay to violate a certain law? What are the risks and costs of taking a certain course of action?

Metaphysically speaking there is no evil in man. The essential parts of man are those features without which a man would not be a man. These are the parts that form what we call human nature. If any of these essential parts were missing, there would not be a man at all. A rectangle that is missing one of its sides is not a defective rectangle; it is not a rectangle at all. Man as man is good. Being good, he is open in his action to good, since evil or lack cannot be a motive or desire. If we deny this fact, we thereby deny morality as a domain of human life. If we deny that man always makes free choices with some good in view, then we either reduce morality to a set of rules that demand our blind obedience or we include in our morality a place for a deliberate consent to evil. Both of these positions are unacceptable. Each man is the author of his own decisions, and as their author he is responsible for these decisions.

While good is the motive of action, it does not follow that everything a man does is good and that there is no place for evil. Reality is composed of many aspects and contains many potentialities, and the structure of reality permits loss and lack. Change is a part of the potential and composite structure of reality. Change is a passage from potency to act. What was only a slab of marble becomes a statue of Hermes by the work of the sculptor. All the sculptor does is to remove parts of the marble that were not needed for the statue. While the slab loses some material, it becomes something beautiful. No one would say that it is evil that the slab of marble is made smaller, but when a dog loses a leg in a fight with a wild boar, that is something evil for the dog. Why is this? The dog has a leg by nature. The leg is not an essential part, that is, a dog without a leg is still a dog, but it is an integral part. Because of the loss, there is the lack of a proper good, and so it is an evil. The whole course of nature involves a certain degree of evil, because for one living being to survive, another must lose some of its parts or even its life. If one animal is going to eat, another may have to lose its life.

When we consider man's action, we see that the problem can be reduced to the following terms. The problem concerns the kind of good that a man chooses, the way that leads to the good, and the other goods that are rejected in the choice of one particular good. There is no other approach. When we obtain one good, we are always rejecting some other good. No one person can do everything at the same time. He cannot eat, sleep, learn, write, read, swim, sit and stand all at the same time. Also, we cannot always acquire the goods we choose without conflict; for example, in order for us to eat, plants and animals must lose their lives.

The fundamental problem that faces man is not how he can avoid all evil in the broad sense, for this cannot be done, but what kind of good he should choose and what particular kind of evil he cannot permit. Man is not faced with a choice between good and evil, but between one good and another. The choice of a particular good is only connected secondarily with evil. When we say that man must choose between good and evil, we are using a kind of mental abbreviation. No one chooses evil as evil.

To unravel this abbreviation, we must consider the hierarchy of the good. We must know what sort of good each thing is, what sort of good can be sacrificed for the sake of other goods, and what sort of good cannot be sacrificed. This also concerns how the good is obtained. If we want to enter a house, we can either knock on the door or we can remove the door from its hinges. The end is the same, but the method differs. The sphere of human choice is difficult because man only chooses what is good, and each good, as good, is attractive in some way. However, the attainment of a certain good may involve some evil. A man makes an evil decision when he sacrifices a higher good for the sake of a lower good, whether this is by destroying the higher good or failing to realize it. We may illustrate this idea. If I am eating dinner and someone in danger calls out for my help, the act of eating dinner is not evil in itself (after all, I am prolonging my life by eating), but it is evil to continue eating at that very moment because I would be lacking a sense of responsibility for a human life in danger. I can always eat later.

While these are obvious things, we may easily slip from a simple explanation to a justification of our actions. When we say that the motive of every action is a good, we are explaining why every action is performed. An action is not justified simply because the ultimate motive of the agent is good. An action is only justified when the chosen good does not upset the hierarchy of the good. A man may find an answer to every objection, but not every answer is a justification.

All our decisions and acts must be ordered in such a way as to respect the hierarchy of the good. The top of the hierarchy is the good in itself. This is a good that we should not use merely as a means but that we should always see as the end and purpose of what we do. If we treat the good in itself as a means, we are undermining the entire hierarchy of the good. Then a moral evil appears, namely a lack of respect for the good in itself. When we choose something that undermines the objective hierarchy of the good, we choose an illusory good — something that only appears to be good.

Study and Reflection Questions

1. What motivates human acts?
2. Explain why evil cannot be the end of human action. Give an example.
3. Defend this statement: Good and not evil is always the purpose of human activity.
4. If every act is chosen for the sake of the good in it, how does evil result from some of our choices?

Supplementary Readings on Human Acts

Aquinas, Thomas. *Summa Theologiae*, I-II, q. 1.
Aquinas, Thomas. *Summa Theologiae*, I, qq. 48-49.
Aquinas, Thomas. *De Malo*.
Pieper, Josef. *Reality and the Good*.

2

The Hierarchy of the Good

We said that everything that appears before us as an object of desire or action is a good. We also know that different things are not one and the same good. Exercise, art and learning are different types of goods. We are faced with the question of whether these goods are radically different from each other, completely separate and autonomous, or whether they are somehow connected. Does each of these goods have its proper place in a larger order and hierarchy? If there were no connections between them, then it would not matter what man desired or chose. The whole problem of morality would vanish. However, we do not need to consider the question very long before we see that there are connections between various goods, and that goods are arranged in a hierarchy.

If I am hungry, I must find food. To get food I go to the store, and for that I need money. Here many actions and their corresponding objects form a whole, governed by a single good or leading purpose. This good is not the act of purchasing in itself, or even eating, but it is the desire to preserve my life. The other goods are merely goods as means to this end.

Our lives do not consist only in staying alive. We like to occupy ourselves with a great variety of activities, and these may take the form of work or recreation. One person dedicates his life to science, another cultivates the earth, another writes stories, and another manages a company. In each of these domains we find many complex activities ordered to some purpose. Our purpose may be to discover new truths, cultivate better crops, create works of art, or maximize profits. At the same time, none of these occupations stands alone. Apart from his career or occupation, a man seeks enough to eat, to start a family and to put a roof over his head. He makes friends with whom he will spend his free time pleasantly. Each man organizes all these things for his own sake.

While each of these spheres of human life has its own specific end, is there still one end to which all the others would be ordered? There is one source of action, and that is man himself. It is a man who cultivates the earth, studies and writes. But to what purpose? The fact that man performs various activities shows that man is a potential being. That is, man does not possess that which he desires, and he acts in order to acquire certain perfections and skills. In this case, man is not merely the source of action, but also the purpose. If he makes a discovery, it is not so that he can lock it in his desk, but so that he may live in the light of the truth. If he tills the earth, it is to provide himself and his family with the means of life. If he makes something beautiful, it is so that people may admire it.

All these threads of human activity start from man and return to him. When they return, they are developed and enriched, and so man himself is enriched and lives more fully. This should not be understood merely in a material sense, as if it were a process of absorption, or literally like spinning thread, because man is a unique being. Man cannot be compared to the other beings we know from experience. In order to understand this, we must take a closer look at the structure of reality, and this will reveal to us the objective foundations of the hierarchy of the good.

The most fundamental manifestation of being is the concrete thing that exists on its own account. In philosophical language this is called a substance (*substantia* in Latin, *ousia* in Greek). Examples of substances in this sense are an actual tree, a cat, a lion or a man. We distinguish a substance from accidents, such as color and length, that do not exist on their own but only exist in something else. All the substances we know always exist with certain accidents. The tree is green and thirty feet high. The cat is gray and weighs twelve pounds, it runs, and so forth. An accident cannot exist without a substance. If there is running, then someone or something is running. If there is a weight, then something has a weight. If there is white, there is something white. The dog does not have to sit, but may lie down instead. The dog does not need to be three feet away from its master, but it can be closer or farther. All these accidents flow out of their substance. The accidents originate in the substance and exist for the substance. Man is not for the sake of eating, but eating is for the sake of man. The tree does not exist for the sake of its color, but the color exists for the sake of the tree. If we reverse this order, we are not taking into account the structure of reality, for when a substance perishes, then its accidents perish with it. As long as the substance exists, it provides a field for the appearance of various properties and activities. The accidents, then, are a good for the substance.

It is obvious that accidents are subordinated to substances, but it may not be so obvious that substances themselves are arranged in a hierarchy. However, if we compare the life of a plant with the life of an animal, we can begin to understand the hierarchy of being. A plant takes in nourishment, grows and reproduces, and these functions are referred to as vegetative. An animal also performs these vegetative functions but has cognitive functions as well. Not only does it take nourishment, it also sees its food and pursues it. The animal also experiences nourishment at a sensual level. Animals are receptive and can be taught many things. We see clearly that the life of a plant and the life of an animal are not life in the same sense, but that the life of an animal is at a higher and richer level.

Just as the life of animals is at a completely different level than that of plants, so man's life is at a higher level than that of animals. Animals have senses and are guided by instincts beyond their control. Man has senses but he also possesses more. He has the power of reason, by which he is open to the knowledge of all that exists. He has the power of the will, which empowers him to love what he wants to love. Man not only sees but also understands. He not only desires, he also chooses. These two powers — reason and will — must be immaterial, and hence spiritual, because they function in a different way than do the senses such as sight and hearing. That which is specifically human in man's activity is always marked by this immateriality. One sign of the operation of our will is human language. Our language is a set of conventional signs. Natural signs are signs that have some natural connection with what they stand for, as smoke is a sign of fire. The barking of a dog is also a natural sign because the dog cannot devise different ways of signifying its reactions. The connection between a conventional sign and its designate depends on free will. The signs of human language have a general content, rather than concrete particulars. Our concepts are the first signs, underlying the spoken or written words, and they have a dematerialized content. Moreover, a man directly touches reality in existential judgments and as a result is able to transcend himself in a way that other animals cannot. He touches not only the reality which surrounds him, but his very self. Only man can say, "I am." Only man can refer to himself as "I."

Cognition is not merely a medium that appears as a stimulus to action (as the sight of an antelope will be a stimulus to a hungry lion). For man, cognition may become an end in itself. We want to know in order to understand and to become wise, even when we gain nothing else. Human love goes beyond the love of self. We are open to love other human beings, whether we merely wish them well or seek their friendship. Moreover, our love may reach out to God, as we see in religion, which is intimately joined with all aspects of human life.

We may consider art as a spiritual activity. Art does not merely serve our immediate needs, but works of art from past centuries or even millennia still arouse our admiration, as if they have lost nothing with the passage of time. There is an immaterial aspect in all we do, and this is a sign of the part our spirit plays in what we do, how we act, and what we make. Only man knows that he knows and that he is the one who knows. Only man knows that he loves, and he can even love his own act of loving. At the same time he can love himself as the one who loves and knows. Acts of knowledge and acts of love can penetrate each other only because they are immaterial. The eye sees, but it does not know that it sees; however, I know something intellectually and at the same time I know that I know.

If acts of intellectual cognition and acts of love are immaterial, then the faculties from which they arise must also be immaterial. A material faculty, that is, a faculty that governs a physical organ, cannot produce from itself an immaterial act. Not only does the eye not see that it sees, but it is limited to certain aspects of reality, such as color, shape, and magnitude. The eye does not perceive the objects of the other proper senses, such as sound or odor, nor does it understand what it sees. By his intellect, man can know anything, both the objects which are proper to the senses, and that which makes a particular thing to be what it is. A man can construct a concept that virtually includes everything, and this is the concept of being as being. Materiality is connected with limitation with regard to place, time and concreteness. Intellectual cognition and its object do not need to be connected with any particular place. A circle is a circle no matter where it is. Intellectual cognition also does not need to be connected with time. Time is the measure of change with regard to "before" and "after," but the contents that our intellects grasp are unchanging. For example, our concept of triangle does not change. Clearly concepts do not exist in time or space. We have never experienced concepts concretely, but we know them intellectually. The contents of intellectual cognition are also general because I may predicate the same content of many different concrete things. For example, I know what a dog is apart from particular dogs, and I call Rover and Misty dogs. In acts of intellectual cognition and in acts of love we experience something immaterial in us, something which not only presupposes the presence of the two immaterial faculties of intellect and will, but which in turn must have being in something still more fundamental. We call this underlying reality "the self" and we refer to it when we say "I." I experience myself as the subject that performs the most varied acts: spiritual, psychic, and physiological acts. (Note that the term "psychic" is not used here to mean anything extraordinary, but simply the acts of man's soul and mind, which is called his *psyche* in Greek.) This subject, which traditionally has been called the soul, organizes this flesh to be my body. Out of this subject arise the various particular faculties, and the subject has been traditionally called the soul. The soul of an animal or plant is completely material, since everything that plants and animals do is performed by their material organs. Man's soul must be immaterial, since it is the subject for both material and immaterial acts. The soul exists in a primary way and organizes the body. The body only has a secondary level of existence. In the case of animals and plants, existence belongs immediately to the composite being. When plants and animals disintegrate physically, they cease to exist, while man is immortal. Our reason can tell us very little about immortality — only that the soul cannot be destroyed when the body disintegrates because it is incomposite, immaterial and possesses its existence directly.

Gradation and hierarchy are found not only between accidents and substances, but also between different substances. If to be a being is to exist in oneself and not in another, then the highest form of being cannot be an accident that exists in a substance, nor can it be a substance such as a plant or animal that exists in material and in a body. Plants and animals are limited *in their being* because they cannot exist without a body, and *in their function* because all their vital operations are tied to some material organ. Only man rises above materiality. Man is not absolutely immaterial, for many of his activities have a material character, but some of his activities are purely spiritual. These are immanent activities, such as the experience we have of what each of us calls "I," which is the subject of so many different acts, but which is not identical with any of them. What is called "I" is not a part of that which is identified as "mine." My hand, my foot, even my feelings and my thoughts, are not the same as "I." That which is called "I-myself" transcends all these other things. In this way, man appears not only as a substance, but also as a person. A person is a self of a rational nature who possesses existence. A person is a being in himself, a full substance.

As a person, man is a complete being; that is, man is a being who cannot be reduced to part of a larger organism. Man is already a whole. He cannot be reduced to a species, nor can he be regarded merely as a part of society. Animals and plants exist for the sake of their species, but with man it is the reverse. Society exists for the sake of man. Man does not exist for the sake of society.

As a person, man has the highest position in the hierarchy of substances. For this reason, lower substances are ordered to him. The whole earth, even the whole material universe, plants and animals, are for the sake of man. Man does not exist for the sake of nature, but nature exists for the sake of man. Man is the good and end in this hierarchy, although man must use his reason and exercise responsibility when he chooses how he will order these various goods to himself. However, it does not follow that because man is the good and end he may then do whatever he wishes. Man is capable of destroying all the forests on the planet and poisoning all the rivers. Such activities would not only be an attack upon nature, but upon man himself. Man has the responsibility of respecting the hierarchy of goods.

When we say that man transcends the natural and material world, and that the material world exists for the sake of man, we seem to be depicting man as a god. When the Greeks and Romans made their heroes and leaders into gods, this was called apotheosis. In a way, when we think of man as a person who transcends nature, this is a kind of apotheosis, but it is not treating man as if he were the one and absolute God. Man is not God. Yet as a personal being, man does infinitely transcend the world of nature, and at the same time man is destined to be united with God. If we deny man's transcendence we also thereby destroy the real hierarchy of being and good. The hierarchy of being and good is the foundation for a normal and rational human life, at both the individual and social level.

In order to establish the hierarchy of goods as objects of our action, we must correctly understand man's position in the world. If man is a person, he must always appear as the end or purpose of our actions. In many cases one person is subordinate to another in some function, such as the division of labor in a workplace, but such subordination may occur only on the condition that both parties truly consent. The subordinate recognizes that his particular role perfects and benefits him; for example, his work provides him with a livelihood, and he agrees to take on this work. We do not ask a horse whether he prefers to pull a plough, or whether a plant likes its flowerpot. On the other hand, if anyone's personal good is at risk the good must be preserved, because each man is unique as a person. In a machine, one bolt is as good as another. We may choose between soup and salad at lunch. We may choose between several applicants if we are hiring a secretary. However, one man cannot be replaced by another. Each human being is a unique and unrepeatable person in himself. As a person, no one can be reduced under any circumstances to a mere function or activity. Each man is a substance, and the highest substance that appears in our experience. The field of human moral action is defined by the good of the person. Any activity that would disturb the good of the person would be a moral evil. Any activity that respects the good of the person is a moral good.

What kinds of good does man seek? Traditional philosophy mentions three basic kinds of good. While we may classify some goods in more than one category, and in some cases we may be unsure how to classify a particular good, the division of goods into three kinds is still useful, even if a logician may find fault with the

[margin, left: so are animals and plant]

[margin, right: wrong; not only persons but every Kingdom]

classification. Reality is rich and analogical, while logic deals with ideas that are simple and clear. We must be careful not to pass over the richness of content and detail that makes the real world so difficult to understand because we prefer the simplicity of logic.

The first good is the pleasurable good (*bonum delectabile*). This is a good that is desired with a view to an activity that is pleasurable in itself. Someone may eat without thinking of nourishment, but because he likes to eat. Even if he has eaten enough, he may continue to eat.

The second good is the useful good (*bonum utile*). This is a good that is a means to an end, a good that serves some other good. For example, eating may be a means both of satisfying hunger and of seeking pleasure. The good as a means may serve the third kind of good.

The third kind of good is the authentic good (*bonum honestum*). This is a good which is an end in itself in an objective sense. Its goodness is not merely the result of our inclinations, as is the case with the pleasurable good. Only a person can be an authentic good, and so man is such a good. A man is a good that we may love in itself, which is why we desire that he lives well and that things go well with him.

These three kinds of good overlap each other. The authentic good may be both pleasurable and useful. If someone has a friend, then spending time in friendship is pleasant, and the friend may do many good things for us. Someone may drive his car for business purposes and also find driving a pleasure. There are also times when the goods are in conflict, however. There are situations in which we endure sorrows for the sake of friendship. We also may lose our property and even our lives for the sake of friends. Then we see not only that friendship is an authentic good, but also that pleasure, usefulness and the authentic good do not always coincide.

Neither the pleasurable good nor the useful good are in themselves evil from the moral point of view. They become evil only when they are put in the place of the authentic good, the good of the person. When does this take place?

The division of the three goods is largely a theoretical division. It serves merely to help us find our way among the various goods that we seek. In reality, these goods rarely appear in pure and unmixed form. All the more, we must be careful not to overstep the boundaries that divide them. We must be careful not to replace an authentic good with a useful or pleasurable good.

We all know that farming and business are useful goods, but if our character is suited to these occupations, we may also find them to be pleasant. The pleasure we take in eating is pleasure in a narrow sense, but the pleasure we take in our livelihood often is broader and it involves our entire personality.

The farmer does not cultivate the earth merely to maintain his family, but also out of a fondness for the earth and for his work. The owner of a company does not only think of money, but he also likes to solve problems. He enjoys meeting people and going on business trips. It is at this point, when we are involved in our work and enjoy it, that it is very easy to forget about the most important good, which is the authentic good. The farmer may lose himself in his work and forget about raising his children properly. The businessman may allow himself to be drawn into some dishonest dealings. The athlete in his desire for victory may resort to performance-enhancing drugs at the expense of his own health. With the exception of extreme situations where we clearly see what is good, in the normal course of human life the most

Connection is what is the most important [handwritten marginalia]

Our actions are only a means to [handwritten marginalia]

common reason why a man departs from the authentic good is that he finds himself too involved in some particular task. He is focused on one thing, and all his attention is on how to do things most efficiently. Our actions are only means to an end, and we must constantly step back and look at the big picture to see whether our actions are ordered to the authentic good. We make efforts to become good at what we do, to acquire practical skills. We also must make efforts to have the proper attitude toward these skills.

Another way to divide goods is into external and internal goods. External goods are outside of man, and they are not an integral part of man. The most familiar external good is property. This may take the forms of tools, land, houses or factories. In a certain way, friendship is the most excellent of all external goods, but friendship ultimately involves a contact between souls, and so it is close to what is within man. Friendship, then, is at least in some respects a spiritual good. We sometimes describe a friend as "another self" or "a second me." Saint Bruno was able to say truthfully that he loved King Boleslav of Poland as he loved his own soul, and even more than life itself.

The internal goods are a real part of man. The first is health of body, which consists in the normal functioning of our senses, the ability to move about without pain, and the general integrity of our body. The other internal goods are closely connected with the life of the person as such. These include the many skills that are called virtues: artistic ability, moral virtue, the mental prowess involved in learning, for example.

There is also a hierarchy among these goods. External goods in the strict sense, that is, material goods, are in the lowest position. Property brings us many benefits, but property is not an end in itself, it is valued for the sake of something else. Money enables us to live comfortably, travel when we wish, spend time doing what interests us, and help the poor. These things are more important than property itself. Property serves these things.

Although we often say that health is the most important thing, it is not the most important. Health becomes very important to us when we are sick, but when we are in good health we often do not think of health. Health is good because the healthy man can do things without hindrance. The healthy man thinks less of health and more of the things that keep him busy. Today, however, we see two extremes: people who disregard their health by consuming junk food and living unhealthy lifestyles and those who are so consumed with health that they experiment obsessively with the latest health products.

There is also a hierarchy among the various kinds of skills and virtues. Moral virtues are not ends in themselves, although that is what the Stoic philosophers taught. The moral virtues are to the soul as health is to the body. The role of the moral virtues is to safeguard the good of the person, which would be in constant danger without these virtues.

In turn, many of the arts could not exist without this principal good. Some arts are concerned with useful goods, such as bridge-building. Others belong to the aesthetic sphere, such as sculpture, painting and poetry. Under the influence of romanticism, many began to treat art as if it were an end in itself. There were several reasons for this. Art was regarded as the expression of a quasi-divine creativity. Art had a function in the realm of truth and knowledge. When art revealed the beautiful, it required the viewer to assume a contemplative attitude for its own sake.

This view of art is both untrue and dangerous. Man is not the creator. He does not give existence to the objects he produces. Man's products exist by virtue of the existence of the raw materials that he uses. Without paint and canvas, there can be no painting. Without wood or marble there can be no sculpture. Works of art also depend upon the existence of man. The work of art requires the emotional and cognitive acts that a man directs toward them. In turn, truth in art is truth in a secondary sense, even in an improper sense. The first concern in art is to produce a certain arrangement of content that will arouse pleasure, even if this is mixed with unpleasant moments. Truth, on the other hand, consists in the agreement of our cognition with some real state of affairs that is ultimately based in existence. The contents of a work of art are not real but intentional, that is they exist inside the human mind. Finally, beauty in art is not an end in itself, but serves something beyond itself. Beauty in art is beauty for the sake of man, so that man may admire it. Moreover, the beauty of art would not exist in any way if there were no men to appreciate it.

An integral part of art's beauty is our love for our own act of beholding; not merely a certain arrangement of contents, but the act of beholding itself. "Beauty is that which, when seen, pleases," said Thomas Aquinas. A culture of beauty cannot be created without man, since beauty is an integral part of his acts. We must remember that the beauty of art is neither a real being, nor is it man or God.

The next set of virtues or skills we shall consider are associated with cognition. The rhythm of modern life, the development of technology, and the universal search for profit have had the result that man no longer knows how to place a proper value on the things that are most valuable. These are things to which we aspire by nature, without which our life as persons could never develop. The life of the person is unimaginable without cognition. No matter what a person does, he must engage in knowing. Even when we think we are doing nothing, our eyes still see and our ears still hear. Our thoughts are in constant motion. Not only do we know what is, but also what was and what will be. We are also emotionally involved in our knowledge. Not only do we know the world by cognition, but by cognition, we are present to ourselves and for our own sake. And when love has a role in cognition we are also present for the sake of others.

Many people think that a person who seeks knowing for the sake of knowing is alienated from life in some way, that real life consists in being busy with eating, business and recreation. However, cognition, if it is truly cognition rather than a retreat into a private realm of one's own concepts and abstract speculations, allows us to take possession of and experience all reality. Aristotle said that in a certain way the soul becomes all things by knowing. A stone is closed within itself. It neither sees nor hears. It makes no difference to the stone if someone strikes it with a chisel. The life of a plant is a more expansive way of existing. Life flows through a plant, consisting in the real assimilation of water, minerals and energy from the sun. The life of a plant is broader than that which surrounds it. An animal not only assimilates food, but by means of its senses it interiorizes a certain larger section of reality. This is an intentional interiorization, different than taking in food. When the animal takes in food by eating, the food is destroyed, but when he takes in something by seeing it, the act of seeing leaves the object unharmed.

By means of his senses and his intellect, man can take in all reality and live in a more noble way. It is a more noble life, because it is a more spiritual life. A man is present to himself in a spiritual way, and he is present to others in friendship. This is a sign of the interiorization that is unique to man. This interiorization appears in a special way when our acts become virtuous. Man is enriched by interiorization. He is not locked within a limited material existence, but he is open to all reality. Cognition, then, as a certain act or function, is the highest manifestation of man's personal life. Cognition can serve many ends, but it is not exhausted in such ends. All the other ends that cognition may serve always lead back to cognition as an end in itself. It would be absurd to put oneself entirely outside of oneself, whether it is in property, or even in the body. The human person must return to himself in cognition as the subject and self that is open to reality. In our acts of cognition that are directed to objects, there is a reflection of ourselves as knowers. In this reflection there is a complete return to ourselves. This is so whether this reflection is fully intended or merely accompanies our acts of knowledge.

There are different branches of knowledge, and each provides us with a special skill in looking at reality under one or another aspect. The biologist, the physicist and the psychologist all investigate something different. Over all these sciences there is one science that bears the rather mysterious name of metaphysics. Metaphysics is not a science about spirits. It is the science that investigates reality as such. It is concerned about being, not insofar as this being is a horse or that being is inorganic, but insofar as it is a being, that is, something real. Another name for this science that is more familiar to us is wisdom. The wise man is one who knows not only how a thing performs, but also understands why. The wise man knows the causes, not just any causes, but the ultimate causes. These are the causes without which there would be no reality.

What do we hope to gain from metaphysics when we are considering moral problems? We have already drawn upon metaphysics when we analyzed the structure of being, when we discussed substances and accidents. Now we will go further. What does it mean to be a being? To be a being is not only to be a man, for a plant and a brute animal are also beings. To be a being is not

Omg this book is so fucking dumb...

only to be measurable, because there are some things that cannot be measured. To be a being is not necessarily to be a material being, because there are also immaterial beings. To be a being is to exist, for without existence there would be nothing. When we examine the existence of everything around us, then we say with amazement that none of these things, including ourselves, has to exist at all. They come into existence and go out of existence. It does not matter whether the term of their existence is one day or five hundred years. Existence, then, cannot belong to the essence of the beings we encounter in our experience, because if it did, these beings would have to exist by necessity. If they do not exist by necessity, what is the reason for their existence? The reason could only be a being whose essence is existence, who alone exists by necessity and is the cause of the existence of all beings.

In philosophical language we call this the Absolute. In religious language we call this God. God, the Absolute, is the reason that explains the existence of everything that is a being. If the existence of contingent beings is not necessary, this means that if they exist, it is by virtue of a free creative act. God wills that something exists. That which is willed is good. Every being, then, is good by virtue of its participation in the creative act.

The Absolute is the foundation for understanding the entire hierarchy of the good. Insofar as man is a rational and free being that is open to immortality, God provides the clue that makes sense of the hierarchy of the good. All the good that we struggle for can be lost in one moment. We could lose everything in a robbery, a fire, or by our own death. The most important thing in human life is to gain wisdom, the loving contemplation of truth. Not everyone is a metaphysician, but each person must be open to wisdom because it is the ultimate perspective of human life. How could it be otherwise?

The end and purpose of human life is the good according to the measure of the personal being, and this is the spiritual good. We can possess the spiritual good by spiritual acts, that is, by acts of the intellect and will. If the absolute God is a person and we exist by his power, then spiritual union with God must be the single end and purpose of human life. Any attempt to replace the real spiritual good with ideas such as justice, equality or freedom is a kind of mockery, because these are abstract concepts and nothing more. It is nonsense to live and die for the sake of concepts. Justice, equality and freedom are in fact noble, for they are immaterial, but they are intentional beings that exist only in the mind. They are not real substances in the same way a person is. The end and purpose of man's life must be a real and personal good.

The goods that appear before us are not equal. Our task is to know what kind of good each thing is and to treat it accordingly. To discover that God exists is not the same as to know Him directly, because God transcends us both in knowledge and being. Religion is the practical application of metaphysical knowledge in our daily life. When people search for meaning in their lives, they most often look for answers in religion. Religion provides the believer with moral guidelines, but religion as such is not the foundation upon which ethics is built. Religion is based on the grace of faith, but not everyone has faith. Furthermore, it is paramount for believers to understand ethics because it allows people of diverse religions to share a common ethical code. The foundation of ethics is our natural ability to use our reason and to understand reality, which includes the hierarchy of the good. The foundation of the hierarchy is God, the Absolute, but even before we understand this, we see in our normal life that there are some goods that must be treated as the good and end because they are a personal being. Morality is characterized by a proper respect for these goods.

Study and Reflection Questions

1. Briefly explain the differences among plant, animal and human life.
2. Defend this proposition: The human being is both material and immaterial.
3. Name and explain the three types of goods.
4. Explain the hierarchy of goods.
5. What type of goods are the following:

Shelter	Courage	Physical strength
Clothing	Artistic talent	Manual dexterity
Food	God	Handsomeness
Sex	Piety	A Picasso painting
Marriage	Wealth	Scientific knowledge
Friendship	Family	Culinary skill

Note that many of these fall into more than one category of good.

Supplemental Readings

Aquinas, Thomas. *Summa Theologiae,* I, qq. 75-102.

Aquinas, Thomas. *Summa Theologiae,* I, q. 5.

Adler, Mortimer. *Intellect: Mind over Matter,* pp. 41-53.

Bonnette, Dennis. *Origin of the Human Species,* pp. 69-74.

Fernández, Aurelio and Socías, James. *A Basic Course on Moral Theology: Our Moral Life in Christ*, pp. 27-30.

McInerny, Ralph. *A First Glance at Saint Thomas Aquinas,* pp. 113-122.

3

The Moral Being — The Decision

The term "decision" comes from the Latin *decidere*, which meant first "to cut apart" or "to slice," and secondarily it meant "to decide." Cutting something in two is a fitting metaphor for what happens in a decision. A woodcutter stands before a log. He can swing the blade of his axe in any place he chooses. A man faced with a decision also has many possibilities for action. What he finally chooses cuts away all the other possibilities. At the same time his action is directed toward one thing and away from others.

The axe of the woodcutter has only one blade to strike the log. Our choice or decision has two blades: every choice determines both the object and ourselves. When we make a choice, we are not merely changing things, but we are also changing ourselves. When we resist something that poses a danger, we become courageous. When we give back something that belongs to another, we become just. It is no wonder that the decision is crucial for man's moral life. By our decisions we shape ourselves.

The decision is a very complex act. A man is often aware of the importance of the decision in a crisis, when existence is at stake and it is a question of "to be or not to be." It may be our own ex-

29

istence, or someone else's fate that is in our hands. These are what we may call existential moments. At such moments, a man must exert his reason to the maximum. He must make his will firm and decide whether he is going to choose one thing or the other, whether he is going to say "yes" or "no."

Situations such as war, concentration camps, economic recessions and political crises force people to make very difficult decisions. Such moments also occur on a personal level, as when someone is considering marriage or a religious conversion. The person faced with such a decision knows that the decision will weigh upon him for the rest of his life. Although he can seek the help and advice of others, he is ultimately the only one who makes the decision, and no one else will do this for him. The decision is more than anything else an internal and personal act.

A man needs more than a formal education to develop skill in making decisions. He must also mature. We should not demand that children decide everything for themselves, because there are many things they do not yet understand. For this reason children are surrounded by the protection of their parents, relatives and schools. Sometimes, old and ill people also need such assistance. There are also some people who are adults as far as their age is concerned, but who have the attitude of children. They refuse to recognize that the time has come for making decisions and taking responsibility. Normally, a man knows that he is the author of his own decisions and that no one can dispense him from this duty. There is no way to escape decisions. Even to refuse to make a decision is a decision. Even someone in the army or a religious order must first make a decision as to whether he will put himself in a situation where he must obey a superior. Although every decision is like a weight or a burden, we may compare this weight to the ballast in a boat. It is better to accept the burden of decisions than to justify our inaction by claiming to be victims of circumstance. If we deny that each man is the author of his own decisions, we upset the moral and legal order, and in turn the proper order of society and man himself. The decision more than anything else reveals that man is a person, a sovereign subject. Not everyone can be a scientist or scholar, nor can everyone become a concert pianist, but each and every one must make decisions.

Decisions are omnipresent in human life, not only in moments of crisis that call for great decisions, but in ordinary moments when decisions are very easy to make. As long as we are conscious, we are faced with various possible courses of action and we must choose between alternatives, even if one of the choices is not to act at all. Often enough we feel no need to deliberate. The good we should choose and the means to it seem obvious, and so we follow a course that we know by experience to be secure. Some people regard daily life as a mechanical process where decisions have no part. We cannot agree with this. We always have the choice of abstaining from activity. The mechanical model of daily life is misleading, especially when we are dealing with real beings, and not mere artifacts. Whenever we choose something, we must always consider whether the good we choose involves something evil.

Every good is a good in a new sense. A great pianist might perform the same composition a hundred or even a thousand times, but each time it is a separate and new performance. This is all the more true when we are dealing with acts of greater moral significance. We make these decisions in response to the actual course of life, and this has not been pre-established like notes in a musical score. Something unexpected might always happen to change us or the situation. Decisions are always present in our conscious life.

It is difficult to analyze the act of decision because of the many factors that enter into it. Some of these factors can be seen at first glance, but others must be brought to light by a deeper philosophical examination.

Every decision is made with something in view. The decision itself is seen as a good, as something worthy of our desire. Not all goods attract us, but only those goods that are known to us. If I am in the forest gathering mushrooms, I will pass by a large and delicious specimen if it is hidden from view under a pile of leaves. On the other hand, I may see a certain good and yet not want it. I may want something else, or else I simply do not have the inclination at the moment. No particular individual good can compel me to desire it. If I want it, it is because I want it. If I do not want it, it is because I want not to want it. This is because the will is an immaterial power that is open to many different goods, and it can choose from among them, even choosing not to choose any of them. Psychologists have devised many experiments to undermine the belief in human freedom by showing that there are many determining factors behind our actions. Such factors may be subconscious, or at a level above consciousness. However, hypotheses must yield to facts. The fact is that each of us experiences freedom within himself. In the face of this fact, we must treat psychological determinism for what it is, an unproven hypothesis that is in conflict with our experience.

I am the one who selects the motive for my choice, and I see this from within myself. Seen from the outside, my choice might seem part of a chain of events that is strictly determined by cause and effect, without any room for freedom. Freedom, however, is within man. It does not reside somewhere outside of him. Freedom cannot be observed in a microscope and cannot be revealed by any psychological test. Freedom is not destroyed by customs or the milieu in which a man lives. It is not destroyed by a man's genetic code, even if one's genetic code strongly affects one's character and inclinations. A man can rise above all these determining factors. He is always capable of saying "no." He can bring about changes in his surroundings. He can improve the customs he has learned. He can work on his character, and he can find an outlet for his inclinations in the good. There is only one condition: he must want this. Without this internal desire, not only is it difficult for us to change, but we will not even be inclined to take advantage of opportunities when they present themselves. That is why happiness most often comes to those who take action and seek it, while people who constantly complain about their difficulties often pass over many opportunities to solve their problems.

The object of our decision is always some good that we know and desire. We may ask whether there is some pressure from the good itself or from our intellect and will that inclines us to seek one good rather than another, or whether it is matter of indifference, and so it would not matter what we chose. Each man experiences that there are certain goods to which he feels a greater inclination or desire, while other goods do not interest him. One man may like to write thick books, while another is distressed if he must write a short letter.

Our subjective desires have an objective basis. If a man is a being that is in some respect in a state of potency, the good is what can perfect his potencies and lead them to act. Potencies are not mere possibilities — they are determined in some way even if they are not yet full realities. One result of this determination is an inclination associated with a potency. Sometimes this determination is great and takes the form of talent or genius. The good that attracts us is in some measure connatural to us. This good perfects us in a certain aspect, and so our will is inclined toward it.

Normally we choose what is suited to us. We engage our will and our cognitive powers toward such a good.

At what moment does a decision become a choice with a moral character? Are we also somehow predisposed to this sort of decision? If the various objects of our desire are not one and the same good, then there is a certain hierarchy. We can understand this hierarchy, and so each of us can see in himself the good of his own person, the violation of which would be something evil. This predisposition takes the form of the conscience.

The conscience is not a mysterious power that exists and acts from some point outside ourselves. It may seem to be a thing simply because we refer to it by a noun. The term *conscience* is from the Latin term *conscientia*, which can be broken down into *con* — with, and *scientia* — knowledge. In the primary sense, our conscience is the state of our mind as we weigh our decisions according to the criteria of moral good and evil. In a secondary sense, it concerns the acts that follow from decisions we have already made.

The voice of conscience is not the voice of some spirit or god, as Socrates described metaphorically when he said he was guided by a spirit that he called a *daimon*, but it is an act that goes along with other acts. It may seem like a mysterious voice because it appears independently of our will. In great works of literature we often see heroes tormented by the reproaches of their conscience, even though they would much rather be free of such torments. They might forget what they have done by surrounding themselves with friends and immersing themselves in festivities, only to be tormented by their awareness when it is all over and the conscience reasserts itself without mercy.

When philosophers explain how the conscience operates, they tell us that there must be a spiritual foundation deep within us that enables us to evaluate our actions in terms of moral good and evil. The conscience must be an expression of knowledge of natural law. In intellectual cognition, when we know an actual concrete thing, such as a tree or a dog that is before us, we see the thing through the prism of first principles. These principles are the principle of identity, non-contradiction and the excluded middle. When I see a table, I know that it is a table (the principle of identity) and not a non-table (the principle of non-contradiction). Likewise, when I evaluate a decision I have made, I perceive that it is either in agreement or disagreement with the first principles of natural law (namely, "do good and avoid evil"). Every man understands the first principles of natural law, even if he does not always reflect actively upon what he understands. The intuition of these first principles is called *synderesis*, which also could be described as the primary and original level of conscience in man.

We shall speak more of the natural law later. It is enough to say now that it expresses the right of each man to life, to the transmission of life and to personal development in the truth. If any of our decisions violate this, whether it is a question of our own rights or those of others, the voice of conscience reproaches us.

We have a natural predisposition to know moral good and evil but the conscience can become deformed or even dormant because of a faulty upbringing or education or a depraved will. The man affected by this escapes the orbit of morality, and he becomes a moral cripple. Since each man is born and develops in a particular society, it is difficult for him to resist social pressures. This is especially true in totalitarian systems where everything has been organized to corrupt man. In the Third Reich and under communism, people actually lost the ability to distinguish the reality of good and evil. Even in non-totalitarian systems, certain forces like the media have the power to distort or silence the conscience.

In much of Western society and increasingly in other parts of the world, young people are shaped and influenced by pop culture which blurs the boundaries between right and wrong. In such a situation, people need more than their native common sense in order to overcome the moral damage, for common sense is also corrupted. They also need religion with its divine authority.

It is easy to observe how all the liberation movements organized by people living under the yoke of totalitarian governments have begun from a growth of religious awareness. When those in power, fellow students, schools and even one's neighbors are repeating lies, the man who still has some remnant of conscience active finds himself afraid to trust in his own reason, and he seeks the help of God. While this might seem like an extreme situation, this is how hundreds of millions of people have lived in the twentieth century, and many still live in the twenty-first century.

Every one of us has the natural potential to develop our conscience, but in each case the conscience must be properly formed. This formation requires more than personal effort. Social institutions, the family and religion also play important roles. It is not always easy to understand the real and appropriate good and the proper means for attaining it in the many concrete situations of life. Life is rich in variety, and reality is complex. Each man is constantly learning over the course of his entire life and cannot avoid making some errors in judgment.

What is the most important element that makes something morally good or evil? We might be inclined to regard the action that results from our decisions as the most basic thing, and so we say that someone has acted well or badly. Sometimes we may say that someone has bad or good thoughts. We may say that someone has bad or good intentions. We say that a person had good intentions when they wanted what was good but things did not turn out as planned. While these moments are obviously important, none of them are the most important. We must find the moment that best expresses our autonomy and sovereignty. We are looking for something without which morality would dissolve into a net of determining factors. Unless we find what is essential, all we will see is a collection of factors, some of which depend upon us, and others which do not. When we focus on those factors that are beyond our control, we might be led to think that we are not responsible for our actions and that there is no such thing as moral good and evil.

Moral good and evil cannot refer primarily to actions, because actions are performed externally. We must take external reality into account, but what is outside of us is not completely under our control. What if I have decided to help someone, but at that moment I suffer a heart attack or someone suddenly attacks me leaving me unable to move? It is always possible that something unforeseen will prevent us from acting or interfere with our actions.

Thoughts by themselves do not always result in actions. Some thoughts even occur against our will. Other thoughts are merely hypothetical experiments, as when we consider various scenarios, as we consider what would happen if we acted a certain way. Finally, there are good intentions. We know the familiar proverb that the road to hell is paved with good intentions. While good intentions are certainly precious, a good intention may be far removed from a good action, and may even be in conflict with a good action, and we have every right to be indignant when someone knows what is good, even wants what is good, but then does something else. Good intentions by themselves are not enough.

If we cannot find the critical factor in actions, thoughts or intentions, what is left? We are left with the decision. The decision is the key to our moral life, and it contains the essence of moral good and evil. Our decisions are completely under our control and we are fully responsible for them. A decision is not yet an action, but it is more than a thought or an intention. It is the final act preceding the action, and at the same time it is the culmination of all the thoughts and desires that preceded it.

When we make a decision we are presented with our many thoughts and desires, and we pick one desire and the thought that accompanies it. A desire is always a desire for something, and that thing must be known to us. Since we are faced with the choice of the proper action, the action must be determined in a concrete way before it begins. Nothing results from what is indefinite. I may be deliberating whether to attack another person or not. If I decide to attack him, then I must choose whether I will strike him with an axe or a knife, because I cannot strike him with both at the same time. I may finally choose the knife and decide to strike him. I do it! The deed has followed the decision.

We find the actual moment of decision very satisfying on one hand but also very difficult on the other. It is pleasant because each of us sees himself as a sovereign master or king who is not subject to anyone else when he makes a decision on his own. The decision is also a very difficult moment, for we are concerned about the possible outcomes of our action. We want to achieve a certain good, but we also know that there is no guarantee of success. Many doubts may arise. Have we thought everything out in detail? Could we have prepared better? What if circumstances change? We cannot always postpone a decision. Good things will not wait for us to make up our minds, so we must make a decision despite unforeseeable difficulties.

When is a decision morally good and when is it morally evil? A decision is good when it is in harmony with a fitting good, or that which is truly good for us. It is not enough for the good to be fitting, we must also know that it is so. It is our conscience that informs us whether the good is fitting. The essence of the moral good is the agreement of our decision with our conscience. If my conscience tells me that something is good, and I decide to seek this good, then there is a moral good. If I decide to seek something in disagreement with my conscience, then there is a moral evil. This is the only way to explain moral good and evil. If we tried to separate the decision from the conscience, and base the harmony of the moral good on the relation of the conscience with the purely objective good, how could we be responsible for an agreement or harmony that we didn't know?

We must make our decisions in harmony with the good as we know it, and not merely the good in some general sense. The result is that even if our conscience is in error it imposes a moral obligation upon us. Sometimes our knowledge is incorrect, or our conscience has been badly formed by factors beyond our control, and then we bear no responsibility. We must follow our conscience, because it is the only moral compass we possess. We must defend the right of conscience in order to defend the autonomy of man as a person. Even when our decision seems like a mistake to others, there is no moral evil if it is in harmony with our conscience. On the other hand, a man is morally responsible for his decisions even when his action has been hindered by external causes. We see clearly here how the legal order differs from the moral order. In general, the law of the state punishes crimes but not decisions. The state punishes someone not for the decision to steal, but for the act of stealing. On the other hand, moral evil is in the decision itself, whether or not the thief carries it out. The act of theft remains a moral evil whether someone else knows about it or not. If a decision is not in conflict with the conscience, then there is no moral evil. Moral evil appears only when a man understands and recognizes that something is evil. When a judge passes sentence, he considers the public good more than he considers the good of the person he has found guilty. Even if the criminal does not think that his action was immoral, he still receives a sentence.

Matters of conscience, particularly someone else's conscience are delicate and need to be handled carefully. Conscience is the forum where each person knows that he is personally responsible. No external punishment can equal the internal punishment that a man suffers from his own conscience. For this reason, the legal order is secondary to the moral order.

The drama of man's moral life is principally within man. Within himself a man gathers the forces of his will and intellect in order to make a decision. Within himself he sees that it is in harmony or not in harmony with the appropriate good. His actions start within him. Within himself he feels satisfaction for having chosen the good, or he feels pain for having chosen evil. Making decisions is an integral part of what we are. The world of nature is free of moral problems, but before us the way is open to the authentic and lasting good. We travel this road as we search throughout our life for decisions that are right. We always have the opportunity, despite our mistakes, to find the right decision and follow it, even if it is as simple as saying "yes" or "no."

Study and Reflection Questions

1. Why is the moment of decision a moment of pleasure and anxiety?
2. Think of a decision you made today. What was the good you chose when you made your decision? What other goods did you not choose by making this particular choice? How will this decision affect you today, tomorrow or next year?

3. Make a list of all the factors that may have influenced a person to lead a life of violent crime. Include external (political, economic, social, familial) and internal (biological, mental, characterological) factors. Given these factors, does this individual have the freedom to choose for or against each violent act he commits? Why?

4. Explain what formation of conscience means. Give an example of how our contemporary culture might malform a conscience.

5. Explain why the moral good or evil of something cannot be determined primarily by the person's thoughts, wishes or external actions.

6. In which of the following scenarios is a *moral* evil committed?

   a) A woman pushed a child over the guardrail of a bridge as a result of which he fell into the water and drowned. Later, it was discovered that she had been trying to save his life by pushing him out of the way of oncoming traffic.

   b) John knows that it is wrong to lie but he believes he will get into trouble for not having his assignment done on time. He therefore decides to lie to his teacher about why his assignment is incomplete.

   c) Jane believes that taking someone else's belongings without permission is stealing, even if it involves something small and inexpensive. One day Jane found herself short on stamps and stationery for her personal correspondence, so she helped herself to some from her employer's supply closet. She told herself that it wasn't such a big deal because everybody else does it.

Supplemental Readings

Aquinas. *Summa Theologiae*, I, q. 79 aa. 12-13; I-II, 1. qq. 9, 20.

Aquinas, Thomas. *De Veritate,* Vol. II, q. 16-17.

Fagothey, Austin. *Right and Reason*, pp. 207-223.

Fernández, Aurelio and Socías, James. *A Basic Course on Moral Theology: Our Moral Life in Christ*, pp. 67-84.

Newman, John Henry. *Grammar of Assent*, pp. 105-112.

Williams, Thomas. *Building on Solid Ground: Authentic Values and How to Attain Them,* pp. 118-146.

4

The Mode of Human Conduct — Areteology

It sounds old-fashioned to speak of the virtues today. We might associate virtue with the heroes of legends and myths. We might think of ideals that rose out of the imagination and genius of masters such as Homer. In the works of Homer, Nestor is the ideal of a prudent and foresighted man. King Agamemnon, the Greek king who leads a great alliance, turns to Nestor for advice in moments of difficulty. Odysseus is quick-witted and thinks things through. He is able to find quickly a cunning solution to achieve his purposes. The heroes of myth and legend are distinguished in each case by one dominant virtue, though they lack other virtues.

The fact that we still read Homer three thousand years later shows that we still regard virtue itself as something universal to humankind. However, when people hear of virtue, they often have a negative reaction. The philosopher Schopenhauer remarked that virtues came to be less valued as social conditions changed. In the life of royal courts, and later in bourgeois society, the classical virtues were supplanted by a sort of conformity that made many concessions to men's vices and faults. Another reason why the vir-

tues have come into disrepute is that some spoke of the virtues as
if they were ends in themselves, and the virtues were treated like
a treasure that had to be carefully guarded. The Prussian system
of education was famous for this attitude. It aimed at breaking a
man's will and individuality in order to make him suitable material for the military or civil service. The Prussian philosopher
Immanuel Kant provided a philosophical argument for this regi-
mented attitude when he wrote that true morality must involve
something unpleasant and that it must result only from a sense of
duty. He thought that if a person found pleasure in doing something, the pleasure lessened the virtue.

Modern psychology on the other hand, tends to reduce the
virtues to habits and acquired reflexes, psychological dispositions
by which we perform certain actions with almost no awareness.
Just as a smoker mechanically reaches for a cigarette, so the virtuous man performs his virtuous actions like a sleepwalker. It is not
surprising that we have seen a reaction against this idea of virtue.
In recent decades people have imitated the heroes of Hollywood
films and television. Their model is someone who is spontaneous
and disregards the possible consequences of his actions. He loves
novelty and is proud of being original and uninhibited. However,
from a philosophical point of view, virtue is very important for
human moral life. It is all the more urgent since in our times we
have forgotten what virtue really is. If the decision is the foundation of moral good and evil, then each man should have the right
moral disposition to recognize the real and fitting good and the
strength of character to pursue the good. Each man is unique and
unrepeatable, and the good never appears twice in exactly the same
form, so we need not worry that the cultivation of virtue will reduce the moral life to a rigid plan. Every man must be prudent
and brave in his own way.

The Greek term for virtue was *areté*. This term appeared in Homer's works where it referred primarily to courage. Of all the virtues courage was the most highly praised since it was the most necessary and obvious virtue in war. The Latin term for virtue is *virtus*, and it also referred primarily to the virtue of courage (the term is derived in part from the Latin word for man — *vir*). At the same time, virtue was not restricted to courage but also included all a man's abilities and skills. Virtue included not only his moral abilities, but also his artistic skills and cognitive knowledge.

The virtuous man might seem like an unattainable ideal, like a marble statue of a mythical hero decorated with a golden garland. The virtues might seem to exist only in a world of pure ideas. We might admire virtues from a distance, meanwhile thinking that they have nothing to do with the routine of our daily lives. This would be a mistake, because virtue is most important in the twists and turns of daily life, where it gives us the ability to recognize and do good and avoid evil. Virtue lives in the active life, not somewhere in the clouds. Virtue can be found in our actions as we face the challenges of real life. The acts of virtue might be varied, but the goal of virtue is one — to foster and protect the human good. A lack of virtue or the possession of vices endangers the human good.

We should not treat either virtues or vices as absolutes. We should not treat them as important for their own sake. We should value them only insofar as they are ordered to the human good. If the virtues help us to make the right decision they are good, otherwise they are not virtues at all but vices, leading us away from the right decision.

Our decisions are free, but we always make them in a certain context. The context is not only objective, but also subjective, deep within us. We must develop what is within us so that our inner self inclines us to the right decisions.

Which virtues do we need in particular spheres of life? Every man performs a variety of activities. These include physiological, psychological, and spiritual activities. We walk, eat, love, learn and produce. Our performance of these activities presupposes that we possess the proper powers for performing them.

We walk by the use of our legs. We see by the use of our eyes. We think by our intellect. All these powers are powers of one subject. In a strict sense, the legs do not walk, but the man walks by using his legs. The intellect does not think, but the man thinks by the use of his intellect. Since all these powers belong to the one subject, very often the activity of one power is connected with the activity of another. I walk somewhere because I want to walk, which requires the power of my will. I know where I want to walk, and this requires the power of my intellect. There are also many activities that are not personal acts in the strict sense but are what philosophers term "acts of man." These are activities that we perform without conscious intervention, that is, without the will and intellect acting as intermediaries. These include physiological activities such as the beating of our hearts and the operations of nerves and the liver. In some cases these physiological acts go hand in hand with our personal acts and decisions. Our stomachs digest food automatically, but we decide what and how much we eat.

The sphere of our senses and feelings is partly dependent on our will and partly beyond the reach of our decisions. Each of the sense organs has a specialized function. The eye sees, the ear hears. We may choose to look or not to look at something. We may choose either to listen to someone or to ignore him.

The intellect and will are immaterial powers. The intellect enables us to understand, and the will enables us to want and choose. These powers differ from all the others because they do not have any specific material organs. They are spiritual. If they did possess material organs, they would be limited. The eye is limited because it sees only color and shape. The ear only hears sound. The eye does not see sound, nor does the ear hear color. The intellect is not limited in its ability to know. Even if we recognize that something is unknowable, we still know it as unknowable. Likewise, the will transcends all specific desires and appetites as it places us before the good as such. A desire by itself is not enough to make us seek something. We must want it with our will if we are going to move toward it. Even if we are extremely thirsty and water is within our reach, we can choose not to drink. Something may be repugnant to us, such as the taste of bitter medicine, and yet we take it when we understand that it is good for our health.

The most fundamental difference we can see between the natural world and man is our possession of these two immaterial powers that have the immaterial soul as their subject. To live as a human is to live according to reason and the will. We cannot do otherwise, even though we may employ our reason and will imperfectly. While the other animals are guided by instinct, we do not have a rich endowment of instincts, and each activity demands that we make an effort to understand and make a decision. We always face the danger that our reason does not know the truth, and our will does not always pursue the proper good. Animals can be completely spontaneous in their behavior because in most cases instinct guides them infallibly. A human being must deliberate before he makes a decision so that the good he seeks does not turn into something evil. His chief task is to live a human life, and this happens when he lives according to reason. Man's fundamental good is to live according to reason.

Only reason tells us what is objectively good and in what measure it is good. We evaluate both the things that attract us and the functions we perform. The pleasure that accompanies eating is not an infallible sign of the objective good that comes from nourishment, because we can approach food with a hearty appetite even when eating would be harmful for us or when we have already eaten too much. When we become sick we may realize that we have not used our reason properly. If we cease to use our reason in the proper way to recognize the objective human good, we will fall.

What is the role of the virtues in relation to our will and reason? The virtues are developed skills of the particular powers or faculties. When the virtues are developed, the faculties perform in such a way that they are best ordered to the proper objective good recognized by our reason. While our internal organs perform their physiological functions by themselves, our other faculties cannot achieve their proper level of performance by themselves, but often resist the essentially human good. We must have dominion over our faculties in order to achieve their optimal performance (*optimum potentiae*), the fullness of perfection. The perfection of the faculties is not for the sake of the faculties, but we seek it with a view to the good of man. We do not train our stomachs to take in as much food as possible, but only as much as our organism needs for health. This reasonable limit has been known as the golden mean.

The golden mean is not a geometrical middle point, as when we find a point halfway between two extremes, but it is the mean of reason, which finds the best state with a view to the human good. If a full bowl of food is sitting in front of us, our golden mean is not to take exactly half, but to take as much as is most healthy for us. Sometimes we may take the whole bowl, sometimes half, and sometimes we may take nothing at all. If we eat nothing, it may still be the mean, that which is best for us. There are times when even eating a little would be too much, as when we know that a certain food makes us ill. The golden mean is defined by our reason, not by the thing.

The development of our particular powers should lead to their being obedient to reason as we achieve the proper mean. The proper development of a man's powers leads to a moral condition where the man possesses the ability to act on his own in accordance with the moral law. The Greeks called this the *hexis prohairetike*. We cannot allow our faculties to become completely mechanized, because we may develop bad habits that rule our actions without thought or decision. We must make a constant effort to recognize the good, because the mean may be constantly changing. We must make a new decision each time, because we are able to choose between many things and different measures. When we have acquired the proper virtues, we can pursue the fitting good easily and quickly, and even with pleasure, even if our action entails difficulty and pain at the beginning. An action is virtuous not because we must face something unpleasant, but rather because it is aimed at the proper good. Virtue does not consist in a heroic effort to conquer ourselves, but in pursuing the good in the most efficient way. When our character is developed by virtue, the result often is that we find pleasure in pursuing a difficult good that would otherwise cause us pain. Virtue is not an elegant cover for vices or bad decisions, nor does the moral good consist in proper manners. The moral good depends upon our internal development and right decisions.

All the spheres of human personal life require development, and in all of them virtues are necessary. Some virtues belong only to the order of knowledge. Every man knows and learns, but not every man is a scientist. The mastery of any scientific discipline requires specific skills. The painter, sculptor and engineer require different sets of skills. The virtues of the scientist are dianoetic virtues, and the virtues of the artist and creator are poetic virtues. Other virtues develop our moral conduct, and these are the specifically moral virtues.

The task of the scientist is to learn the truth in a skillful manner. The task of the artist is to produce or create something. The task in the moral order is to foster the human good, especially when this good may be in danger. There are four basic moral virtues. The first is *prudence*, which consists in the development of reason so that it is able to recognize the good for what it is. The second is *temperance*, which consists in the ability to master our feelings of pleasure and pain, since these feelings may lead us away from the objective good. The third virtue is *fortitude*, by which we master our feelings of fear and pain, since these feelings may also lead us in the wrong direction. The fourth virtue is *justice*, where the will is trained so that it looks not only for our own personal good, but also for the good of other people, who as people have the same rights as we. Justice is the constant will to give to each what is due to him.

The four virtues are connected with each other, but they are not equal. In order of importance, they are prudence, justice, fortitude and temperance. Most of the time people see the relative importance of these virtues by common sense, even though they do not have a deep understanding of what the virtues are or how to acquire them. Sometimes people confuse virtues and vices. They may say that a cunning man is wise or prudent. We have a wealth of words at our disposal to describe personal character, but we often forget the objective meanings of these words or their history in classical culture. A character trait is a virtue only when it is ordered to the proper good. Cunning is a sign of intelligence, but it is not a virtue because it is directed toward something evil. Other character traits such as fidelity are morally neutral. We can only decide if fidelity is virtuous if we know to whom a person is being faithful. Fidelity in an evil matter such as a criminal's fidelity to his gang is something evil. When we face a choice between personal loyalty and complicity in some evil deed, we should suspend our loyalty and withdraw from the relationship. The best way to avoid this situation is to be careful about making promises of loyalty in the first place, but that is a matter of foresight, which is part of prudence and is based on much accumulated experience.

Many modern writers are able to reach and influence a large audience because of the mass media. Even if they aim at entertainment, movies and television shows can have a strong moral influence on their viewers. However, the writers of these dramas often do not have a proper education in ethics and as a result they spread their own confusion to others. Contrived trivial problems are sometimes presented as grave moral dilemmas for the sake of drama and excitement. Moral dilemmas have their place in drama, but a writer should know how to present them properly. As Aristotle said, a small mistake in the beginning will lead to large consequences in the end. Small mistakes are often subtle and difficult to avoid, and so require greater vigilance. Newspaper journalism is another source of confusion. Columnists may juggle terms with the deliberate purpose of confusing the reader, so that he will either agree, or else doubt his own good judgment.

The classical conception of the virtues is necessary and it should have its proper place at the foundation of a good education. When we recognize the virtues, we are on the road to a true education and a sane culture.

Study and Reflection Questions

1. What is the attitude toward virtue in our society today? Try to think of specific examples from your own experience.
2. How did the Greek view of virtue differ from the one presented in this chapter?
3. How does one determine if a particular trait or characteristic is a virtue or a vice?
4. How do the virtues help us?
5. Explain the golden mean. Think of an example of your own.

Supplemental Readings

Aquinas, Thomas. *Summa Theologiae,* I-II, qq. 49-66.

Aquinas, Thomas. *Selected Writings of St. Thomas Aquinas*, pp. 75-113.

Aristotle. *Nicomachean Ethics*.

Fagothey, Austin. *Right and Reason*, pp. 224-237.

Gilson, Etienne. *Moral Values and Moral Life*, pp. 134-159.

Plato. *Protagoras* and *Meno*.

Redpath, Peter. *The Moral Wisdom of Saint Thomas: An Introduction*, pp. 67-70.

THE VIRTUE OF PRUDENCE

Philosophers in the Western tradition called prudence the chariot of the virtues, in Latin *auriga virtutum*. This metaphor has its roots in Plato's dialogue, *Phaedrus*, in which the course of human life is compared to a chariot pulled by a team of horses, one black and one white. The white horse symbolizes our good inclinations and the black horse symbolizes our evil inclinations. To reach his goal, the driver of the chariot must know how to control and guide his team, especially the black horse. Only the driver knows where he wants to go, and the burden of guiding the team falls upon him. The role of the driver is even more difficult if he knows that in reality the inclinations are not good or evil in themselves. Each inclination has the potential to be either good or evil. The good or evil of the inclinations depends upon how they have been developed and whether they are guided properly. If the inclinations are to be developed and guided properly, he must know what is good and what is evil, and not merely in a general sense, but in a specific way according to his circumstances.

Saint Augustine defined prudence as the ability to know what is good, which we should seek, and what is evil, which we should avoid. According to Isidore of Seville, the etymology of the word "prudence" is from two Latin terms: *porro*, which means *forward*, and *videre*, which means *to see*. The Greeks used the term *phronesis* to describe prudence. Heraclitus was the first philosopher to use this term, and he used it to signify a certain philosophical ability to penetrate constantly changing reality in order to discover the *logos* or law that governs it. Aristotle used the term *phronesis* in a narrower sense when he applied it to moral knowledge. Moral knowledge deals with concrete things and situations that are always changing, whereas philosophy or wisdom deals with the ultimate, general and invariable causes and reasons for reality as such.

To understand better the function of prudence in our moral life, we must first take a broad look at the various activities of reason. The first is knowing for the sake of knowing, which the Greeks called *theoria*. The most perfect form of knowledge for the sake of knowledge is found in science, which concerns that which is general, necessary and unchanging. Science is not interested in the concrete individual as such. The biologist studying a plant does not look at it as a unique individual, but as the representative of a species. When the plant he is studying perishes, he gathers others for his scientific needs. He is interested in discovering the general structure, properties and laws common to all members of a species.

Poetic knowledge is concerned with producing or making something. Unlike scientific knowledge, it is concerned with the concrete individual, for the product is concrete. The concrete individual thing is unique and changing. The species studied by science possesses a certain set of characteristics, but leaves out everything that sets one individual apart from another. The knowledge of the builder or artist cannot be schematic and general, but it must be focused on the concrete.

Like poetic knowledge, moral knowledge also deals with concrete things. While moral knowledge contains and acknowledges universal principles, it is primarily concerned with the concrete good for a particular individual man, not with the good understood abstractly for man in general. Man in general does not have real existence. In the real world, there are only concrete individual people and concrete individual goods. The difference between poetic and moral cognition is that poetic cognition is concerned with the good or perfection of a product or artifact, while moral cognition is aimed at the good of man. Moral cognition requires the virtue of prudence, and poetic cognition requires the virtue of art.

The aim of prudence is the human good, and this is a necessary end. We can never truly doubt that the human good is a necessary end, and consequently we cannot doubt that prudence is necessary. We do not deliberate about the human good because prudence is aimed at happiness, and all men by nature aspire to happiness. Differences of opinion arise when we try to define the good in which happiness consists. Different people have different opinions about happiness. The task of prudence is not to solve this question, for this belongs to the philosophy of man, which is a certain kind of wisdom. Some see their happiness in wealth and others in power, while others think happiness consists in pleasure; however, all agree that man is always the subject of happiness, and all these goods are for man.

We must first know who man is in order to find the right relation between man and these goods. Since man is a subject and person, he must always consider this supreme good while he is seeking various other ends. The primary end is already established. The primary end is the person and subject, but the means to this end may vary. In the course of our life, we act in many different spheres, each of which has its own proper and unique end. For example, the end of eating is to preserve life, and the end of acquiring property is to guarantee the proper conditions of life and to pursue some activity that we have chosen.

Prudence is the ability to know means to the end, the means that will bring us to the end we have chosen. The ends we choose are ultimately ordered to the good of man. Imprudence consists in an inability to find the right means, which is the same as the choice of improper means. One of the vices opposed to prudence is cunning. Cunning is also an ability to discover means to an end, but the means it chooses violates someone else's personal good. The supreme end of prudence must be the good of the person.

Prudential knowledge is a complex process. The first phase is a consideration of the means that we have at our disposal and the means we must try to obtain. The second phase is circumspection, where we try to find the most proper and fitting means. The third phase is prudence in the narrow sense, which coincides with the decision where the person says, "This is the means I choose." Prudence may be destroyed by incompetence when someone does not know how to find the means to the end, by haste when someone grasps at the first available means without due consideration, or by a lack of prudence in the strict sense when someone cannot make a proper decision at all.

Our will has a different role in prudential knowledge and theoretical knowledge. In theoretical knowledge the evidence of things forces us to recognize the truth. I see what I see, and the will has no influence on it. By my will I can deny what I see, but this cannot change the fact that I see things as they are. The only power the will has in theoretical knowledge is not to look at things in the first place.

In practical knowledge the will has a more important role. When I face a decision, my first choice is whether or not I will seek any means at all. I may choose not to seek any means, particularly if this would require effort. On the other hand, I may want to explore various means. At a later stage, even though I may have many means at my disposal, for one reason or another I may not want to find the most proper means. Finally, when I know the most proper means, I may still decide upon another. Prudence depends very much upon the will, both in its preparatory stage and in its most important stage of decision. A good will, a will that is directed with all its power toward the proper good, has a very important role in moral knowledge. By the power of a good will, we will try to gather the greatest possible number of means, to seek the best means, and to choose it. If the will is not upright but depraved, we will direct the process of moral knowledge to agree with a choice of means that is in harmony with our bad will.

A man seeks what he wants to find and passes over what he does not want to find. When the will is wavering, which is a very common situation for all of us, it can undermine all our efforts to know the truth. The result is that our action takes the wrong form. When this happens, someone may be confused by the evil results of what he has done and try to explain himself by saying that his intentions were good. Often his intentions were simply not evil, but not good to any special degree. The Polish writer Sienkiewicz remarked that intentions are not enough, but that one must know how to want, or to put it even more strongly, one must want to want.

Prudence is difficult because it concerns concrete individuals. Individual things and people are unique and different and do not always match perfectly our general conceptions. Our intellect finds it difficult to grasp anything that is not general. Someone may be very adept at working with concepts while he has trouble dealing with real life. The sciences work with concepts and their relations and boundaries. Scientific concepts are very limited and leave out any details that are not of interest to the scientist. These concepts can be expressed in the strict language of mathematics and analyzed easily by computer, but these techniques are not very useful in real life. Strict scientific knowledge does not help us understand and cope with the rich variety and change of ordinary life in the real world.

Someone may have mastered mathematics, but this does not mean that he will know what to do in a situation in real life. A good literary scholar will not necessarily be a good writer. Likewise, a man who knows ethical theory may not know how to apply his knowledge of ethics in real life. Each man must learn prudence and the other virtues on his own, forming himself in the virtues by repetition. This does not mean that he does not need the help of others or a knowledge of theory, but ultimately no one else can take his place in the process of learning. As mature persons we must learn to be prudent. We must have a proper conception of the purpose of life, and then we must know how to find the proper means leading to this end.

It is difficult to be prudent because prudence is a complex virtue. Philosophers in the classical tradition describe at least eight components of prudence.

The first element of prudence is *memory*. As we act, we deal with things that are not necessarily the same each time and which are constantly changing. In order to know the way things are at the present moment, we cannot limit ourselves to the present. We must draw upon the accumulated knowledge that we hold in our memory. Inexperienced people have the greatest problems dealing with human affairs. If they do not have enough experience they may be surprised or puzzled by events. Without experience, we may either be too naive and trusting, or else too frightened of the unknown. In either case, our judgement will be clouded. People who remember that similar events have taken place, and who are able to make good use of their memory, are better able to recognize present events for what they are. We can enrich our memory by reading historical works, for history is the teacher of life — *historia est magistra vitae.*

The second element is *the ability to understand reality*. We often approach reality schematically according to our preconceived notions. This is normal, because the function of our intellect is to generalize. We grasp the most apparent features of things and generalize them. Sometimes we must concentrate and take a closer look at a particular thing, as if we were sinking ourselves into it as we examine something about it that interests us. This is a more perfect mode of knowledge, and this is how we know the people close to us, our animals and the particular plants in our garden. When we look at things from a distance, we see them in terms of general concepts that express what is common to their species or type. In daily life we are not dealing only with people who are close and familiar, but also with strangers who have different personalities and characters. When we are in contact with strangers, we must know how to understand them, which will save us from many misunderstandings and disappointments.

The third element of prudence is *openness to the advice of others*, called *docilitas* in Latin. The English words "docility" and "docile" have come to mean a passive attitude, and so we would describe a sheep as a docile animal. However, the original meaning of "docile" is "teachable," from the Latin *docere* — to teach. Modern educators promote independent thought and originality, and have taught us to disregard docility as a virtue. Each person is ready to defend his opinion to the end, not because it is right, but because it is his. He regards those who ask questions as having no opinion of their own. However, we must know how to distinguish the man who is willing to listen to others from the man who blindly accepts everything that he hears. Docility is the virtue whereby we are able to give an attentive hearing to those who have more experience than we do. This virtue is necessary, because no individual man is able to accumulate so much experience that he can pass a sound judgement in all matters. At the same time, when we pay attention to what others are saying, we decide to what extent we will take their advice. Opinionated people lack docility. They cannot be partners in dialog since they prefer to deliver monologs. A person who is docile in the proper sense will be very interested in what a prudent person tells him concerning important matters. Some religious orders have an ancient rule that the superior must listen to what the other monks have to say, even though only he has the power to make decisions.

The fourth element of prudence is *cleverness or quick-wittedness*, which was called *sollertia* in Latin. This is the ability to see how things or events are connected. The thoughts and intentions of others are often invisible to us. People may intentionally hide their true intentions or try to mislead us. We must try to make an educated guess as to the true reasons behind the actions of others. Otherwise we will often be misled.

The fifth element of prudence is *reason*. This is the ability to judge properly, and here we make use of the rules of logic. If we are students of logic, however, we must remember that the rules of logic are general, but we are dealing with the concrete. In order to judge a situation reasonably, we need more than logic and definitions. There are many circumstances and details that may directly affect our judgement. If we deliberately overlook the details and try to force the facts to fit with our ideas, we become dogmatic in a bad sense. We will be quick to praise or blame others. This attitude reminds us of the sorry tradition of ideological and political struggle, but it has nothing to do with responsible and benevolent moral judgment.

The sixth element of prudence is *foresight*, called *providentia* in Latin. We perform every activity with some end in mind. This end is still in the future, since if we had already arrived at our goal we would no longer be in motion. The end we seek may be to realize something that does not yet exist, or to preserve for the future something that we possess in the present. We must think of the future and we need foresight. Foresight is the most important element of prudence, but it is also the most difficult. We must develop a plan of action for the various situations that might work for us or against us. Many things may happen within the bounds of probability. The past and present are necessary, that is to say, they cannot be other than they are. Future events are not necessary, because they may either take place or not take place. Complete certainty with regard to the future is impossible. We all feel anxiety over the future. The ancient Greeks and Romans sought divine help, and resorted to seers and various kinds of divination. They tried to find signs of the future in the entrails of sacrificed animals and in the flight of birds. If we avoid superstition and limit ourselves to the human means at our disposal, then we should develop our foresight by exercising our imagination, while employing all the other elements of prudence. Very few people exercise their imagination in a prudent manner, and so they are easily surprised by the turn of events. People who have developed their natural ability of imagination are regarded almost as seers. When we read the memoirs of famous people who exercised foresight, or listen to the accounts of such people close to us, we see that they have spent much effort to analyze complicated political or personal situations. Foresight is the most difficult part of prudence, but it is most important for success in our actions.

The seventh element is *circumspection*. Circumspection completes what is lacking in foresight, because even under the best circumstances we cannot foresee everything. We must always make provisions for the unexpected, so that such events will not prevent us from reaching our desired goals. If we are never willing to depart from our plans, then either many events will hinder us, or we will do evil. Our action must be flexible and circumspect.

The eighth element of prudence is *caution*, in Latin *cautio*.

When we prepare for action, we should prepare the means for overcoming possible obstacles. We must forearm ourselves, so that we do not lose too much time and paralyze our action when we meet obstacles.

As we have seen, prudential knowledge is not easy. The eight elements of prudence are not an artificial construct, rather everyone resorts to them spontaneously in real life. However, when people do the right thing spontaneously, they are like gamblers who sometimes have good luck. When we know the elements of prudence, we know that in new situations we should try to foresee events, try to see connections between things, and so on. In this way we will develop habits that will work spontaneously, but also very effectively. It is important to know and apply these elements. Each element of prudence is not equally important in every situation, and if we apply them too rigidly we will seem ridiculous. Nevertheless, we should know them and use them at the proper moment.

What is the connection between prudence and conscience? We defined conscience as the natural ability to know concrete good and evil in a moral sense. What, then, is the use of prudence? Prudence is the virtue of a well-formed conscience.

We should take care to develop our conscience. The conscience is present within us as a certain potential. We must actualize it so that it adheres to the objective good as closely as possible. Since the good is always given to us in knowledge, our cognitive abilities must also be properly developed, and prudence assists in this. Although an erroneous conscience still places an obligation upon us, it is better that it should not be in error at all. Each person should be careful to form his conscience so that it will conform to the objective good with the help of prudence. While we will then make greater demands upon ourselves, we will also have a better taste for life. The knowledge that we have done good gives us satisfaction. Who is more to be pitied than one who lives in darkness? Wise men have said that it is better to be an unhappy Socrates than a happy fool.

Prudence is the light which shows us how to find the proper means to achieve our intended goal. Prudence is a virtue only on the condition that the goal we choose is authentic and the means we choose do not violate the good of the person. Prudence can be directed either to the good of a particular individual, or to some public good, the common good. The people who are responsible for the public good need to have the right predispositions for their work, but not everyone possesses the right predispositions.

If we lack prudence, we cannot possess the other virtues, since only reason can understand the right measure. We may speak of a rule or measure for moral good and evil, but it is not a rule in the strict sense; the man who possesses prudence is himself the rule. The rules for right action are general, but in action we are aiming at a concrete good, and we must be able to understand it. The first step in prudence must be docility, that is, being open to the advice of other people.

We start thinking independently about abstract and clearly defined concepts at a time when we still rely on obedience to others in matters of practical action. It is easier to understand mathematics than to judge correctly about good and evil, because correct moral judgments require accumulated experience and humanistic learning. The current trend in education is to teach the formal sciences and technological skills to children from the beginning of their school years. Children learn more science than in years past, but this is at the cost of another important part of education. Children are spiritually deprived, because their human nature is not properly fostered. They are not properly prepared for living a truly human life. They are prepared to be robots, no longer subjects and persons, but instruments or tools that are easily directed by those above them. To be prudent is to be constantly sensitive to the good of the person. When we are open to the good of the person, we become aware of new levels of authentically human life.

Study and Reflection Questions

1. What is prudence?
2. What is the difference between empirical scientific knowledge and prudential knowledge?
3. Why is docility a necessary part of prudence?
4. Explain how foresight, circumspection and caution work together to help us make prudent decisions.
5. Describe how you would go about developing one of the eight elements of prudence in your own life.

Supplemental Readings

Aquinas, Thomas. *Summa*, II-II, qq. 47-56.
Gilson, Etienne. *Moral Values and Moral Life*, pp. 233-245.
Pieper, Josef. *Prudence*.
Vaske, Martin. *A Philosophy of Morality*, pp. 146-156.

THE VIRTUE OF TEMPERANCE

The foundation of the moral life is the ability to use reason properly. Only in this way can we see the objective and fitting good. A man, however, is not pure reason. He is one being and substance composed of many parts. He possesses many powers, and each of these performs its own proper function. One and the same man walks, eats, transmits life, feels sad or happy, sings, or dances. Reason plays a role in all these activities, but it is the whole man who performs them, not reason alone. When we examine the way animals live, we are amazed at how perfectly they hunt, run and defend themselves, while man is by nature a rather helpless being. Many years must pass before a man learns what he needs to know, and even then he often learns imperfectly. In contrast to the other animals, we do not have instinct to direct precisely the way we act. Some of our behaviors are activated in us by nature when we are newly born, but most of these disappear with time. As a result, we must rely on reason. Only our reason is able to see the end and perfection we should seek. Only reason can produce order within us and preserve the proper hierarchy of goods. We do not intend to glorify reason, because man's reason is relatively imperfect. We are aware of the limits of our reason from experience; nevertheless, it is our highest power. If someone tries to cast doubt upon the power of our reason, he is using reason to make his point. Any critique of reason is also a work of reason. It is better to develop reason than to doubt its power.

In the realm of art, we develop reason for the purpose of ordering activities aiming at the production of some piece of work. In the realm of science, our power to know is ordered to knowledge for its own sake. In the sphere of morality, we use knowledge to bring order to the life of our feelings.

We may wonder how feelings are connected with morality. We have many problems with our feelings. For animals pleasure is a reliable sign of something good, and fear is a reliable sign of something evil. An animal tends to that which is pleasurable and avoids that which is painful. These feelings are also properly tuned or tempered by nature. The feelings of an animal are usually in perfect harmony with real and present good and evil. The good gives it pleasure, and that which threatens it causes it pain.

We know, however, that there is often no relation between what gives us pleasure and what is objectively good. That which is evil is not always painful to us. Even when the good is also pleasurable, the intensity of the pleasure or pain may not correspond to the scale of the good or evil. We must look beyond our feelings to see the real good or evil that corresponds to them. We do not judge our feelings on the basis of some other feeling, nor on the basis of sense knowledge. The only basis for judging feelings is reason. A man who guides himself only by his feelings will sooner or later be lost, and he will hurt himself or others.

Our emotional life is very complex. If we want to portray it accurately, a psychological description by itself is not enough. We must take a broader view. The first thing we should notice is that we can distinguish two movements or attitudes in relation to an object. The first is a movement toward an object, and the second is a movement away from it. Love is the internal source of the first movement. *Love* is an internal principle of inclination to something. The source of the movement away from the object is *hate*. Both love and hate may work at different levels. At a basic sensual level, love can give rise to physical appetites such as hunger, or an emotional attraction, and hate can give rise to feelings of disgust and aversion. At a more spiritual level, love gives rise to a more spiritual desire, and hatred gives rise to a more spiritual aversion. We should emphasize two things here. Hatred is secondary to love. We hate something that is opposed to what we love. In turn, feelings only appear when we know about the object of our love or hatred. We cannot find joy in a thing if we do not know that it is within reach or that we possess it. Likewise, we cannot be sad about something if we do not perceive it as a threat.

There are other feelings called the *irascible* appetites. They appear when it is difficult for us to achieve what we want, or when it is difficult for us to avoid something that we dislike or hate. When the good is difficult to obtain, we experience either fear or discouragement at the sensual level. At a more spiritual level we experience hope or despair. If it is difficult to avoid an evil, we experience daring or terror, courage or fear. In order to attack evil we can elicit the feeling of anger from ourselves.

We must know how to master our feelings, but we must master them without extinguishing them. Plato and the Stoics recommended that we should be completely free of feelings, but this is a mistake. We must use our feelings as energies that can lead us to the good and keep us from evil. We need the virtues. First, we need to know how to master our feelings of pleasure. Second, we must be able to master our feelings of fear. Pleasure can intensify our desire too much, while fear can easily lead us to surrender to evil. We need the virtue of temperance to master pleasure, and we need the virtue of fortitude to master fear.

Pleasure is most intense in those parts of our life where we are closest to nature, that is, where we are dealing with the preservation of life and the transmission of life. Our inclinations to self-preservation and to procreation are the strongest inclinations in us. Before someone begins to ponder the meaning of what he does, what is good and evil, whether life is worth living, what he should study, what profession he should pursue, he is already continuously doing by instinct what he needs to do to stay alive. He eats. Unsatisfied hunger is associated with a very intense pain, while hunger satisfied is associated with intense pleasure.

When someone matures, in turn a strong inclination to transmit life rises in him, and this takes the form of the sexual drive. When it is not satisfied, there is tormenting pain, while satisfaction is associated with pleasure. Poets and people with much experience of life say that when someone does not eat, they are either ill or in love. This should not surprise us. Nature seeks the good of the species more than the good of the individual, and so the inclination to transmit life can overcome the desire for self-preservation. Of course, both of these desires operate in us in a uniquely human manner and not merely as animal instincts, although they are rooted in nature. A man finds his happiness in being a man, not in being an animal.

We learn temperance with regard to eating very early in our lives. We do not acquire this virtue by our own effort alone, but through our elders. Our parents or guardians have the responsibility of training us. They use their reason to provide us with the right amount of food at the right time, and they also teach us how to eat well. By their efforts, they produce in the child certain dispositions that the child will later cultivate by his own thought and effort. The inclination to self-preservation through eating and drinking is very strong and we need to understand the purpose of this inclination and its place in the integral life of man. An excess or defect, where there is either too much or too little, turns against man, and it can affect his health. Sickness can ruin our lives. When people are chronically ill, their illness often keeps them busy. They may be preoccupied with their health, endlessly seeking one treatment after another. Meanwhile, health should enable us to give ourselves freely to the activities we like, whether producing things, learning, or perfecting our abilities. Illness can limit the scope of our activities, or even render us unable to do anything.

Since eating is a human activity, we cannot take too narrow a view of it. While eating has the primary aim of self-preservation, it also integrates the family, neighbors and friends. It can express hospitality and friendship. Because eating also has these social aspects, food and alcohol often are served together. There is nothing wrong with this as long as we observe the proper measure. The proper measure is particularly important with regard to alcohol, which in some cultures is always served at banquets. Not only does alcohol aid the digestion, but as Homer said, it also cheers the mind. The proper measure with regard to alcohol is most important, however, because eating to excess is not as dangerous as drinking to excess. While excessive eating can hurt our bodies, excessive drinking can also cause a total eclipse of reason. The worst evil that can befall a man is to lose his reason, because this degrades him in his inner being.

Eating is connected principally with the sense of touch, but sight and smell play mediating roles. When a cook prepares food, he appeals to the sense of sight and smell to encourage eating. The sense of smell is close to the sense of touch, and for this reason it is very intense, but it is more limited than touch. Sight is closer to the intellect. Sight is less intense, but it is broader in scope. Someone may most easily go beyond the proper measure in eating on account of the sight of food, eating with his eyes, as it were. The aesthetic pleasures connected with sight contribute to the pleasure of eating, and this easily leads to over-eating. The ancient Romans were ingenious in finding ways to indulge in the sensual pleasure of eating. They built rooms called vomitoriums, where the guests could clear their stomachs in order to eat more. This practice was a rather perverse use of reason. Intemperance is not just a problem of the past, however, as the alarming statistics on obesity in the United States indicate. We should remember that the proper measure in eating is not an objective measure derived from the things that we eat, but it is a measure established by our reason according to the occasion, our dispositions, and the requirements of our health.

The inclination to procreate takes the form of the sexual drive. It presents a very complex problem with serious consequences. Here the human good must be safeguarded by the proper use of reason and strength of will. We should emphasize a few aspects of the sexual drive. Since this drive does not concern merely one person, but relations between people and the possible conception of a new human person, it is a very serious matter. Aristotle was one of the few philosophers who was able to perceive things that are overlooked because they are too obvious. He thought that in sexual relations, we temporarily lose our reason. The power of nature and the intensity of our feelings may be so great that reason undergoes a total eclipse. As if that were not enough, man not only tolerates this eclipse, but he ardently desires it. This is not a trivial matter. If culture does not intervene, then the flame of love can set a man afire.

On the other hand we see that sexual maturity appears at the most decisive moment in our life. We have an awakening sense of self, a sense of distance from the world and other people, and we have our first serious reflections upon the meaning of things. At that moment, each one consciously begins to build his own personality. He also begins to absorb knowledge and acquire many skills more intensely than before. His personality is woven like a delicate fabric, and it can be enriched by an increasing sensitivity to culture. The culture he acquires at this time will be with him over his entire life span.

The later tensions he may feel in the area of sexuality will never be as deep or as powerful. If the strength of the sexual drive is set loose too soon, it can destroy everything. It can dull a person's sensitivity so that everything seems to be at the same ordinary level. It can chain the receptive mind to purely utilitarian functions. It can change great pleasure into sadness and apathy, and it can close tight the doors to personal development. A young person does not fully understand this. The fabric of personality is delicate at this time, and he needs the firm and loving help of others.

The inclination to transmit life involves relations between different people, and the most important relation is our relation to the human being who is conceived as a result. Conception is an unquestionable good — a new human being comes into existence. It is unfortunate when the child is conceived by someone too young to take responsibility, or when the parents are not married, for then the child will be unwanted. This situation is only a short step from abortion, which is in fact the killing of a human being. The virtue of temperance has a much greater role in sex than it does in eating. It is not concerned here with personal health, but with human life. One reason for reserving sexual intimacy for marriage is that marriage best guarantees that the new child will receive proper care and that he will have favorable conditions for development. Under normal circumstances, marriage arises from love. Aristotle beautifully described this love as an excess of friendship. The best kind of friendship is where each friend has concern for the good of the other. Friendship in this sense protects man from becoming a mere instrument of nature, which is always a danger. Although some cultures do not disapprove of premarital relations, sexual relations are a very intimate and personal area, and this is very important in forming a long-lasting friendship. Without proper care, young people can lose something of value forever, as the poet Sappho once sang: "Virginity, virginity, where did you go when you left me? I will no more return to you, I will never return."

This problem is not only serious, but also needs to be handled delicately. The problem is one that goes beyond our internal experiences. Unfortunately, sexuality is also exploited in the marketing of political parties and ideologies. Publishers also make fortunes by exploiting our sexual drives. The great torrent of pornography weakens people's minds, depriving them of strength and dulling them, especially in the case of young people. A normal person is strongly convinced that he has a right to intimacy, and that matters of sex are very personal. We do not like the thought that someone else would interfere with this part of our lives or give us commands. It is right that we should feel this way. We should be able to direct ourselves, and then the command to do what is good should come from within us. However, we should know well what we are deciding. The recent phenomenon of high school students taking a voluntary virginity pledge is an example of what we mean here.

Unfortunately, democracy today has lost sight of its historical roots in Western classical culture, and it seems to look more to the barbarians who conquered Rome. The Greeks called the ideal state a *polis*, and today we speak of a republic or polity, where responsible citizens have a vote and have been educated to respect the cultural ideals expressed in the constitution. The same Greeks used the term "democracy" to mean the rule of the mob, or *demos*. This may also be described as the proletariat. Each person may choose what he wants, but what kind of choice is this when he is barely aware of what he should do and what he should choose? When the masses of people have not received a proper moral education, they simply follow the suggestions of the mass media, which is the most organized cultural force in society. Yet freedom does not consist in a man's being able to do what he wants. Freedom in the strict sense is self-determination. We are free when we are able to determine ourselves to act toward an end that we have considered well from various angles, and to use means that we have prudently selected. This is real freedom, not an illusion.

The virtue of temperance only concerns a very small area of our personal life, even if this area is not isolated from the rest of our life. Temperance orders the course of the inclinations mentioned above, so that these inclinations will work for man, not man for the inclinations. Temperance prepares the ground for the development of higher virtues, not only moral virtues, but also artistic and cognitive ones.

Study and Reflection Questions

1. Explain why a person, unlike an animal, cannot rely only on feelings or instincts to judge what is good and evil. Provide an example. How can we help our feelings become a better guide for us?
2. Make a list of human activities or skills that are instinctive and those which must be taught or learned.
3. How might the virtue of temperance help us with respect to eating and sexual expression?
4. Roman nobility held feasts called orgies which involved consumption of vast quantities of sumptuous food and drink, aided by the vomitoriums. How would you answer a Roman who defended his participation in these feasts by saying, "It's a free country and I am free to make my own choice"? Now how would you apply these same arguments about the true nature of freedom and temperance to the sexual excesses in our own culture?

Supplemental Readings

Aquinas, Thomas. *Summa Theologiae*, II-II, qq. 141-170.

Fernández, Aurelio and Socías, James. *A Basic Course on Moral Theology: Our Moral Life in Christ*, pp. 283-299.

Gilson, Etienne. *Moral Values and Moral Life*, pp. 276-287.

Hildebrand, Dietrich von. *In Defense of Purity*.

Hildebrand, Dietrich von. *Marriage*.

John Paul II. *Love and Responsibility*.

John Paul II. *On the Family: Apostolic Exhortation Familiaris Consortio*.

Plato. *Charmides*.

Pieper, Josef. *Fortitude and Temperance*.

Smith, Janet. *Humanae Vitae: A Generation Later*.

Vaske, Martin. *A Philosophy of Morality*, pp. 159-160.

THE VIRTUE OF FORTITUDE

Just as pleasure can pull us toward something that is opposed to the essentially human good, so pain and fear can pull us away from this good. When pain and fear influence us, we may leave our pursuit of the good, and in this way we become subject to evil. In times of war, an enemy may use both ways to undermine our desire to defend the good of our country. An attacker may try to break the resistance of the defenders by bribes and promises, or by threats and torture. Threats result in fear, and torture results in pain, and both can cloud reason and break the will. In this case, the defender needs the virtue of fortitude, which gives him the strength to defend the good in the face of an impending evil.

Fortitude or courage is necessary in many forms and in many situations, not merely in the extreme situations of war. We need it constantly, even if perhaps we are not aware of this. Writers popularize military courage, but they overlook courage in daily situations. However, every day we encounter situations where we must face things that threaten the good, and we must face fear and pain constantly. These daily situations always require fortitude.

Fortitude has two major forms. When we are faced with evil, we have two ways of responding. Evil is not something that exists in itself, but it is something that acts against our good. Something that acts without heed for our good is evil. The first form of fortitude is the best known, and it is the inclination to attack. The second form is more subtle, yet it is higher than the first. It is the inclination to resist, described by the Latin verb *sustinere*. Fortitude inclines us to attack when it appears to us that we can overcome an evil. When this is the case, we build up the energy of anger and we strike. When we think that an evil is stronger than we, then we resist. We suppress our fear and we remain firm in opposition to the evil.

The first problem we face is how to judge the threat. We cannot take the feelings of pain or fear as our guide. We must first master these feelings so that our reason can think freely. Fear quickly steals into the human heart, because we often have much to lose. Aristotle said that such fear is not merely possible, but that we must have fear. After this, we must face the fear with a firm heart. Here we need fortitude. When we have mastered our fear, we then need prudence to recognize the scale of that which threatens us. If it is not great and is within our power, then we should attack it. In this situation we release the appropriate anger that will give us the power to attack. Sometimes it is enough if we simply demonstrate that we are angry. Perhaps today there are few people who know how to be angry in an intelligent way, and so the term "anger" has lost its original sense. When people think of anger, they think of someone who takes offense at small things. When they think of anger, they think of hysteria or of someone who becomes easily upset. Hysteria and irritability weaken someone's ability to act rather than strengthen it. We need fortitude in order to arouse anger in ourselves. It is the feeling that inclines us to fight as the response to fear. We first fear, but after this we must say: "I will not surrender!" Cowardice is resignation and a refusal to attack when faced with an evil that we have the power to defeat.

Often an evil is beyond our strength. In times of peace we may encounter economic, political or cultural pressure. Here we need much prudence to recognize evil, because it is not always readily apparent. It is often deliberately concealed. Economic pressure can appear in the simple form of poverty, but political and cultural pressure are well concealed, as they are prepared by specialists who have money, technology, and the support of large institutions. It is not easy to decipher such evil, for it does not appear as a threat, but takes the appearance of something good. First we must see whether this good is in fact something evil, so that we may properly fear it and think about it. When we see it as evil, we protest against it in our thoughts. At the same time, this internal protest cannot move immediately to anger and attack, because in this way we would not defeat the evil, but at best we would be finding some release. Our purpose must be to defeat the evil, not to indulge in emotional release. Those who create political and cultural pressure have already calculated for angry reactions. They even provide ways for people to complain in public and to unload their dissatisfaction. When people have expressed their dissatisfaction and vented their anger in a futile show of feelings, those who are exerting this pressure can return to what they were doing without opposition. If we are truly courageous and do not consent to an evil that is beyond our strength, we must stay firm in opposition.

Now we see why we need more courage in being firm in our opposition to evil than in attacking it. If we are in the weaker position, we are directly affected by the evil, whereas those who threaten us are in a position of security. They can control and redirect our feelings of anger, and so what we need instead of anger is firmness of purpose.

We must also be vigilant, because there may come a moment when we are in a position to attack the evil. It is very difficult to perceive the right moment, and so the Greeks spoke of the right moment for action as having almost a divine quality. They had one word for time in the usual sense — *chronos* — and another for the right time or opportune moment — *kairos*. The opportune moment is the secret of a successful attack. Unfortunately, we often act too early or too late.

The virtue of courage, conceived as the ability to be firm in resistance, is not only a higher virtue than attack, but it is also more difficult to acquire. Personal effort is not enough. We also need to learn from the example of others, from our teachers and parents, tradition and history. We are rarely able to see very far beyond ourselves, and so we place a greater value on lesser goods that we can obtain now than on distant and uncertain goods. Such shortsightedness weakens the higher virtue of fortitude. Some things require us to look far into the future, at the good of future generations. We may easily despair, become discouraged and resign ourselves to fate. If we do so, we are simply surrendering to evil. There are some situations, such as when one nation is occupied by another, where one generation must pass on hope to the next, and the memory of who they are as a people. Without the element of hope, the memories of the past would be tragic nostalgia.

When we speak of evils that threaten us and of facing evil with courage, what particular evils do we have in mind? In primitive societies, people would personalize evil, embodying evil in particular people or even gods. This would simplify the struggle against evil. If they identified evil with particular people, they could fight against them. If they identified evil with certain gods, they could resign themselves to evil by telling themselves that it was the will of the gods. However, the problem is more complicated than that. There are no evil gods, and man is good insofar as he is man and a personal being. Evil can only appear in the context of activity where certain elements are absent. Evil as a privation appears as the result of a privation in the person who performs an action. The most obvious privation is when one man fails to consider the dignity of another man. Such a person acts as if other people were only tools or means to an end. He uses people arbitrarily, telling others what they may or may not do, and if they resist he might even have them killed. People see that this is evil, and they call their oppressor evil. Yet we must always remember that this is not evil in an absolute sense, but it is an evil that is connected with a certain action, for evil is not a being, a thing or a substance. This is important, because our defense against evil must always be properly directed against evil, not against a being and a good.

The defender's purpose is to cause someone who is threatening him to act in a different way. His purpose should not be to destroy the person who acts against him. If this were his purpose, he would be destroying the good of persons, but even the greatest evil-doer is a human person. It is too easy to kill, but most often this does not solve any problems, because in the place of one tyrant another tyrant rises. Tyrannicide, as one instance of violent means to achieve political ends, only results in more slaughter. We can see this in the history of the Byzantine empire and Russia, where in the struggle for the throne not only were rulers murdered, but whole families were killed as well.

The defender must also show that highest virtue of courage when he faces the fear of his own death. When death is staring you in the eye it causes great terror. When they are in fear of their life, men may agree to all sorts of debasement, whether betraying a secret or blindly obeying the orders of their oppressor. While someone may save his life by debasing himself, this kind of surrender does not solve anything. Every one of us must die sooner or later, and it is not certain that an unjust oppressor will keep his promises when he says that he will not kill us. Often those who betray others in exchange for a promise of safety are killed in any case. A man must master his fear of death and stand firm with courage. This kind of fortitude is an expression of man's transcendence in relation to his own life on earth. The death of Socrates is a beautiful example of this. No matter what he does, no man can preserve his life on this earth forever, so if he is going to be concerned about anything, he should primarily seek to defend his own dignity and his fidelity to the good, to truth and justice. This is his purpose in life. This end and purpose cannot be identified with earthly life. If earthly life were man's end, then man would live only to die. This is an absurdity, all the more since there is a rational basis for recognizing that man is open to immortality by virtue of his possession of an immaterial soul. Although this involves a mystery that can only be unveiled in part by religion and faith, man still has the constant experience that he transcends his body, the world and biological life. We must protect our transcendence as spiritual beings at any cost, but the same cannot be said of our biological life. Man is not called to life as such, but to a worthy life. This worthiness or dignity requires that we do not fear death, that we do not consent to falsehood, and that we do not consent to evil.

Evil can threaten us in different ways, and so there are different kinds of fortitude. We need one kind of fortitude in times of war to defend the common good of the nation. We need another kind of fortitude when we must defend our own life and wellbeing. In such cases where our actions may easily result in the death of another human being, we must clearly distinguish the final and most important purpose from that which can happen incidentally. We cannot have as our end the death of another, but only the defense of the good. For this reason, we rightly say that a person who threatens the life of another and dies when the other defends himself has really killed himself.

Participation in war is a sign of fortitude only when the war is just. In order for a war to be just, it must meet certain criteria.

It must be declared, and the one who declares it must have legitimate authority over his country. It must be for a just reason, and it must always be as a defense against something which poses a real and imminent danger to the common good. The end must be just, that is, the purpose must be to defend the good. There comes a moment when one has an obligation to take part in a war, and this will be explained in greater detail when we discuss the virtue of justice.

Some evils threaten the spiritual good, and then the most important thing is to speak the truth. We have an obligation to proclaim the truth despite persecution, blackmail and any kind of pressure. The real development of the person is based on the truth, and all men have the right to the truth. Deception deadens man. It presents an illusion as a reality. When ideas and lower goods are treated as higher goods, they are an illusion. It is not true that the purpose of man's life is to acquire property or to find pleasure. It is not true that class struggle is the major engine of humankind's development. The dictators in totalitarian regimes try equally to deprive their subjects of personal freedom and to make it impossible to discover or proclaim the truth. In this way their subjects are oppressed in two ways. They cannot do what they wish, and they cannot know where the real good is. It is often the case that a state that has been liberated from tyranny falls into a state of chaos, leading to a new tyranny.

It is not enough to recognize evil. We must also know where the real good lies. We need a proper education. Of all things, truth is to man the most precious, and we should not spare any effort in seeking, defending and spreading the truth. This must be done with prudence. Poland was occupied many times, but each time one generation would pass on to the next the Polish language, traditions and culture in secret. We may remember as well, those who worked to bring literacy to slaves in the American south at a time when this was illegal. The transmission of truth embodied in culture is a most precious treasure. Culture is the work of many generations, and each individual does not need to start from the beginning, but he can draw upon the work of others and develop.

The more educated someone is, the more he needs fortitude to defend the truth, and to avoid selling his knowledge to evil in exchange for a more comfortable life or advancement in his career. There is no sight more worthy of contempt than an educated and enlightened man who has been unfaithful to his mission in life.

The virtue of fortitude is a habit and skill whereby we are able to master our fear and oppose an evil that is attacking a bodily or spiritual good, a personal or social good, and we are able to do this promptly and consistently. This is one virtue that does not give us joy immediately, because it is directed toward evil. Indirectly, fortitude can bring us joy, which comes from the principal end which is the good it defends.

We must understand what it is to oppose evil. To oppose evil is not to return an evil for an evil. Our response to lies must be to speak the truth, not to speak more lies. The purpose in our struggle to defend our own lives cannot have as its end the deprivation of another of his life. Hatred for an enemy must be limited to a hatred of the threat he poses to our good, and it cannot be directed to the man as a man. The value of the human person cannot be reduced to that of being an enemy or a friend.

If someone, despite everything, still harbors doubts about the meaning and value of fortitude, he should ask whether he really loves the proper good. If so, then how can he consent to its destruction? If we love something, we desire that it exist. If we consent to the destruction of the good, this means that we do not love this good, but instead treat it merely as an occasion for love when it is convenient. We then are loving love rather than the good. This is a selfish attitude that is expressed in love for one's own feelings. The brave man, on the other hand, always has in view the proper good. He is not afraid to defend his own dignity or that of others, even at the price of losing his own life.

Study and Reflection Questions

1. Describe the forms of fortitude.
2. What role does prudence play in fortitude?
3. Why is courage in the face of the threat of death important?
4. How would fortitude help us overcome political or cultural propaganda?
5. What are the conditions for a just war?
6. Imagine that you lived in the American south in the era of slavery. What good or goods did slavery threaten? How would you display fortitude in fighting this evil?

Supplemental Readings

Aquinas, Thomas. *Summa Theologiae*, II-II, qq. 123-140.

Fernández, Aurelio and Socías, James. *A Basic Course on Moral Theology: Our Moral Life in Christ*, pp. 256-257.

Gilson, Etienne. *Moral Values and Moral Life*, pp. 276-287.

Plato, *Laches*.

Pieper, Josef. *Fortitude and Temperance*.

Vaske, Martin. *A Philosophy of Morality*, pp. 158-159.

THE VIRTUE OF JUSTICE

We already know that the subject of morality is man as a person. He is a sovereign being capable of understanding and achieving objective knowledge of the good, and he can freely make his own decisions. Since he has these abilities, he must use them to direct his life. He finds help in certain internal habits and skills, such as prudence, temperance and fortitude. There is still one more virtue of man, a virtue which evoked the wonder of poets and philosophers at the dawn of Western civilization. This is the virtue of justice.

Some people say that justice is the rarest thing under the sun. After all, each man seeks his own good and is concerned about himself. If someone in addition has in view the good of someone else, perhaps this is a sign of some unusual heroism, grace or sacrifice. In primitive cultures, justice was most often associated, not with concern for the good of another, but with vengeance and punishment for those who stood in one's way. Primitive people would pray to their gods for vengeance.

Today, unfortunately, we often have the same conception of justice. However, the foundation of justice is neither grace or favor nor punishment. The foundation of justice is to give to each person what is due to him. If justice were nothing but a grace or favor, it would consist in giving something to another which is not due to him. It would be a gesture of giving. If justice were nothing but punishment, this punishment would be conceived as the fulfillment of a desire to make things equal as a consequence of some injury, especially an injury that we have received. Justice in this sense would not be concerned with the good of another, but with our own good.

It is easy to see that both positions are wrong. If a man is truly a person, that is, a sovereign subject, this is the title by which something may be due to him. As a person, he may claim his rights. Each one of us must respect the rights of the person. Every man has a right to the good that is appropriate for him. When man is reduced to being a part of a state or religious organization, like a part of a machine, his rights vanish from view. Then he becomes a nobody apart from the function assigned to him.

On the other hand, we should not treat man as if he were a minor god who distributes goods to others out of grace. In the first case, man is pictured as a servant or a slave, and in the second case he is seen as a ruler and tyrant. Although each man is born, develops and lives in some particular society, he is also higher than society. Society is a relational being, but man is a substance. Ultimately, society is for man, not man for society. Justice must be founded on a perception of the good that is due to man as a person.

Justice appears in the context of social life. Certain philosophers of the seventeenth and eighteenth centuries created the fiction that there was a time when men lived without being organized into societies. Yet man is always born in a certain society where he acquires a language and culture and works together with others. He lives in various societies — his family, his city, his state and today even the entire world as a society — and there he is connected by a network of relations to other human persons.

The virtue of justice causes in us a stable and immovable will to render to others that which we owe them. As humans we are equal to one another, whether we are rich or poor, whether we are educated or not, whether we have authority or not. Each of us is a subject and a person and possesses dignity. When we say that someone is more or less human, we are not speaking of what they are as a substance in their nature, but of how they act. The first and most basic demand of justice is that we respect the dignity of each man. We may not despise anyone in our heart, even our greatest enemy. Such disrespect or hatred may take the form of a feeling of superiority or of holding a grudge against our enemies. It is a sign that we have lost our ability to see reality because of an intellectual, cultural or even religious blindness. We must take special care to avoid this mistake.

In daily life, our respect for the dignity of others is commonly expressed in actions that are part of good manners, such as extending our hand or tipping our hat, as well as greeting others with pleasant words. We should not forget such gestures. While they are small, if they are missing in daily life, their absence harms the foundation of our relations with one another, and we may easily find ourselves treating others as objects or disregarding them.

There are three particular forms of justice. The form of justice that is easiest to understand is commutative justice, which governs relations between particular individuals. We have this kind of justice in mind most often when we say that someone has acted justly or unjustly. For example, we say that someone has provided another with what he owed to him, he has not deceived or cheated others, he has not overcharged others for goods and services. The remaining two kinds of justice are more difficult to understand. The first is legal justice. This kind of justice obliges every human person by virtue of his belonging to a society. Our society can make a claim upon each of us. We call this legal justice because many of our obligations to society, though not all, are defined by its laws. Without legal justice society would collapse. In the third form of justice, society through its legal authorities owes us something, and this is distributive justice. We will examine these three kinds of justice in greater detail.

Study and Reflection Questions

1. Describe two misconceptions of justice.
2. What are the three forms of justice?

Supplemental Readings

Aquinas, Thomas. *Summa Theologiae*, II-II, qq. 57-80.
Gilson, Etienne. *Moral Values and Moral Life*, pp. 246-275.
Plato. *Gorgias* and *Republic*.
Pieper, Josef. *Justice.*
Vaske, Martin. *A Philosophy of Morality*, pp. 156-158.

Legal Justice

Human society may be organized in various ways. The broadest and most complete today is the state. In ancient times, such as in ancient Greece, the state was identified with one city, called a *polis*. The state must be properly organized. It will have a particular political regime and power will be divided according to the type of government. In his book, *Politics*, Aristotle lists six kinds of political organization, and his list is recognized as definitive even today. The first type is monarchy, the second aristocracy, the third a polity or republic. Aristotle says that these are the right and proper forms of government. When they are corrupted, they result in the other three forms: tyranny, oligarchy and democracy (which in classical terminology meant "rule by the mob"). In both monarchy and tyranny one ruler governs. In both aristocracy and oligarchy a certain small group of people holds power. In a polity and in a democracy all the citizens or a majority of citizens exercise power. In the proper forms of government, the rulers are con-

cerned for each man's right to happiness. In the corrupt forms,
the rulers are concerned with their own happiness. The tyrant takes
care of himself, and he thinks only of how others may serve him.
A group of oligarchs tries to organize the other members of society to serve their own private interests. In a democracy, the government aims to please the general mass of people, but not all of
them. On the other hand, where the government is not corrupt,
those who hold power aim at the happiness of all the citizens. A
monarch differs from a tyrant, because the tyrant takes power by
force, while a monarch represents the best people. An aristocracy
consists of the best people from among the class of specially talented individuals, while a republic or polity consists of rulers who
are the best from among the general population. Aristotle thought
that the best system is a monarchy with a system of just laws. He
held that this type of monarchy was the system most capable of
ensuring a happy life. It looked beyond the basic necessities of
social life and provided a life full of "beautiful actions." Happiness is not the same as freedom, although this is a slogan of modern democracy. Happiness consists in the best way of life. Freedom is not an end in itself, but it is a means by which a man might
be able to live a beautiful life. A true monarchy or a true aristocracy worthy of the name tries to produce this kind of life for the
citizens, and it pays special attention to education.

Legal justice takes different forms depending upon the political system. Legal justice may be reduced to two fundamental
obligations that the citizens have: to sacrifice some of their property, and possibly sacrifice their lives. If the state is to function
normally, it must have the proper financial resources, and so part
of the income of the citizens must go into the treasury of the state.
The state commonly obtains this money through taxes. We do
not find it pleasant to pay taxes, but without taxation the state

would collapse. The sacrifice of one's property is an integral part of legal justice, although perhaps "sacrifice" is not the best term. However, this term is commonly accepted in ethics, so we should not change it. It is much more appropriate to speak of "sacrifice" in situations where the state is threatened by economic collapse or war. When the United States was threatened by economic depression following the terrorist attacks in 2001, a small group of Fortune 500 company owners worked together to buy large quantities of stock to try and help maintain the stability of the economy. By doing so, they risked their capital at a time when many people were selling their stocks and exiting the market. Around the same time, a well-known athlete gave up a highly lucrative contract to serve in the armed forces.

Legal justice may also call upon us to give up our life. We must have a responsible attitude concerning military service. Someone may serve in the military as a volunteer or as a conscript, and the terms of military service are legally defined. Over the years we have been surrounded by pacifist slogans. Most often, these slogans were proclaimed by superpowers that actually were inclined to war and used pacifist movements to weaken their enemies. We cannot reject the armed defense of the common good. A normal man regards war with revulsion. War brings death and destruction, but at times it cannot be avoided. The army is necessary to defend the common good. The defense of the common good is the reason for the obligation to serve in the military and to be prepared to give up one's life.

There are times when some people do not see the obligation of legal justice as an unqualified good. This is the case especially when someone lives in a system which, as Aristotle would say, has become corrupt. One cannot understand why it is necessary to part with property and life itself to defend a state that is not organized to provide the conditions for all of us to develop freely and to lead a happy life, and that seeks to profit from its citizens and enslave them. When people see the state as corrupt, they are inclined to avoid paying taxes and performing military service. Perhaps the best example of what legal justice can become when it degenerates is what is often called social justice. While it is called justice, it often is justice in name alone. Its purpose is often not the good of the actual people, even of the so-called working people, but only the good of those who are in power.

Where people perceive that their government is legitimate, they feel that it is natural and good to pay taxes. Such a state ensures the personal security and development of each and all of its citizens. For thousands of years people regarded death in defense of one's native land as an expression of true heroism, and military service was a cause of pride. Today, when computers and atomic weapons are part of the arsenal, the justice of risking one's life for one's country might not seem as obvious, but we must still keep in mind why our native land is worthy of demanding personal sacrifice, even the sacrifice of our lives. The state is a formally organized society that occupies a territory with definite borders, but the fatherland or native land is also a cultural heritage. To understand what fatherland means we must know the culture of which it is the vehicle. This culture is the heritage of many generations. If someone were to limit his life to sleeping, eating, work and play, then the fatherland will not seem necessary to him. If he knows how to draw nourishment from a tradition that he sees as priceless, and he relies on this tradition for the integral development of his person, then he will look at his fatherland with great respect. He will regard his land's traditions as his own, even as a part of his own being, for he was born in this tradition, he grew up in it, and it belongs to him. We may exchange one state for another, but our fatherland, like our parents, is something that is permanently ours. We must know how to hold it in esteem and how to live by it.

The Spartan King Leonidas will always be a symbol of patriotism. He faced the Persian army at Thermopylae with only a handful of soldiers. He was vastly outnumbered, and his entire army of about a thousand men lost their lives. The battle was lost, but the Persians were weakened and lost the war. King Leonidas was not guided by pride, but by love for his fatherland, for he said: "I owe my fatherland more than life itself."

King Leonidas is an example of patriotism, not nationalism. Patriotism grows from a love for one's fatherland, which is a real good. The word "patriotism" is derived from *patria*, fatherland, which in turn is derived from *pater* — father. The fatherland provides us with the opportunity to develop in the truth and the good, whereas nationalism is a love of a nation whether or not there is a real good connected with it. For the nationalist, the nation often means a specific ethnic group, and so his nationalism excludes many of his fellow citizens. Most often nationalism is connected with an illusory good, and we encounter various forms of nationalism in totalitarian states, such as the Third Reich or Czarist Russia. Unfortunately, today the concepts of patriotism and nationalism are confused. Both are regarded as the same thing, and both are regarded as dysfunctional. This attitude robs us of the right to love our own fatherland, but this is an inalienable right. Not only is readiness to suffer death in the defense of our fatherland a requirement of justice, as this is properly understood, but also a love and concern for our fellow citizens and for future generations, that they may have the same share in the good that we have.

Study and Reflection Questions

1. Name and explain Aristotle's six kinds of government.
2. Why does justice demand the readiness to sacrifice one's property and one's life for the state?
3. What is the difference between patriotism and nationalism?
4. Describe one way in which our country provides the conditions for all citizens to live happy lives. Describe one way in which our country falls short of providing all citizens with these conditions.

Supplemental Readings

Aristotle. *Politics*, bks. III & IV.
Gilson, Etienne. *Moral Values and Moral Life*, pp. 309-328.
Maritain, Jacques. *Man and the State*.
Simon, Yves. *Philosophy of Democratic Government*.
Vaske, Martin. *A Philosophy of Morality*, pp. 156-158.

Commutative Justice

Commutative justice concerns the relations between particular individuals. People can be related to one another in many ways, and so commutative justice is also extremely varied. Commutative justice concerns the basic duties we have toward others simply because they are human beings, and the specific duties that we have toward certain people. We have unique obligations toward family members. There are some rights and obligations that are specific to the exchange of goods between buyer and seller. There are certain rights and obligations in passing on the truth. Every man has the right to preserve his life, health and personal integrity. We must respect these rights, and any violation of these rights must be vindicated in justice, although not in the same sense as in the Code of Hammurabi, which contains the principle: "An eye for an eye, a tooth for a tooth." If we follow that principle when we are dealing with someone who has done us wrong, then we will in no way be different from the wrongdoer. In civilized societies, crimes are punished by incarceration, fines, or verbal apologies. Some crimes cannot be requited in like manner, as when someone permanently injures another or takes another's life. Unfortunately, in such cases there is nothing that can undo the harm done. Injuring or killing the criminal does not restore the health or life of his victim. Mutilating or executing the criminal does not make things equal, but such cruel punishments are an expression of injustice. They strike at the right of every man to life and health. The convicted criminal is still a man, and he still has these basic rights.

Commutative justice governs the relations between members of a family, especially between marriage partners. Marriage depends upon the free consent of the spouses to spend their lives together. Their consent implies the promise of complete fidelity to their marital promises, that they will be honest with each other, that they will love each other, and that they will take care of their children.

Commutative justice also governs our actions in commerce and business, and it demands first of all that we be honest. Honesty in business is like arithmetical equality, that a person should give just as much as he takes. This form of justice is easy when the things exchanged are of the same kind. Two men may exchange horses or cars in a very simple transaction. Most often, two parties in a business transaction exchange goods of different kinds, and the only common measure is money. The value of merchandise includes more than its cost to the merchant. It also includes the work of the merchant and his employees, the cost of building and maintaining his store, and a certain amount of profit. Without profit no one would want to engage in business. The buyer pays a higher price for the goods, but the difference between the retail price and the wholesale price compensates the merchant for his work. This is easy to understand. However, profit that comes from interest payments involves further problems. At one time, all lending at interest was called usury. For many centuries usury was regarded as an evil. This attitude to usury had religious grounds, as usury was forbidden in most circumstances by the law of Moses, and it had philosophical grounds. Today, interest on loans is an accepted part of business everywhere.

Aristotle presented the following philosophical argument against usury. Natural things produce a natural increase in the form of offspring, but money does not increase naturally. If a farmer borrows grain for sowing his fields, the grain produces more grain, so the lender may justly ask for the same amount of grain and part of the increase in return. If we consider what money is we understand that money by itself neither increases nor decreases naturally. There are artificial ways to change the value of money, such as the various processes that devalue a currency.

If we understand that money is only an artificial sign for real goods, we can understand why some interest on loans is reasonable. If I have money, I can buy seeds to sow my fields or do something else that will benefit me by its increase. When someone lends me money he is losing the opportunity to enjoy this increase himself, therefore paying him interest would be appropriate. Another factor in interest is that it also includes the cost to the lenders such as banks. Just as the price of goods includes the labor of the merchant, the cost of maintaining his store and so on, the interest that the bank charges covers its costs, including the cost of defaulted loans by a portion of its borrowers.

While we can justify interest on loans when we properly understand the nature and function of money, usury is still a moral problem. Today usury primarily refers to excessive interest rates. The worst example is the loan shark who charges very high rates and backs up his loans with threats of violence. In many cases lenders use loans to control the borrower. When the borrower is unable to repay, he can lose his independence. He can be manipulated and used like a slave. There are moral issues when financial organizations use loans to gain economic and political control over entire countries, especially when they lend to tyrants who spend the money for their own private benefit leaving the entire people to repay the loan and interest.

A borrower also has moral responsibility. If a person uses credit to buy luxuries beyond his ordinary means, he risks his own future and that of his family. Many families have been burdened because of the indiscriminate use of credit by some family member.

Commutative justice also requires that we be just in our speech. The problem of truth and lies is a problem of justice. Speech is a great gift. Speech is a vehicle through which we grow as persons. Without speech, an authentically human life would be unimaginable. The signs that animals use are called natural signs, that is, their meaning is determined by nature. Human speech consists of conventional signs, whose meaning is determined by man's decision. The vocal communications of animals are strictly determined and very limited, whereas man's speech is open and unlimited in its expressive power. Human speech has the potential to express all that is in the reality that surrounds us, and the reality of our inner personal lives as well. We can also speak of that which is not directly knowable but which is the reason for all existence, and without which the existence of the world would be an absurd fact without reason. That is, we can even speak in a meaningful way about the invisible God. There are two basic modes of human knowledge that set us apart from the other animals. These are abstraction and judgment. The result of abstraction is the concept, which expresses certain general contents. The term "man" is the sign of a concept. The concept applies to many different concrete human beings. A judgment is either predicative or existential. In a predicative judgment we predicate a feature or property of a given subject. The predicative judgment is expressed in a simple sentence with a subject and predicate: "John has blond hair," "John is sitting," "John is thinking." The existential judgment does not have a predicate. Existence is the soul of the existential judgment. When we say that John is or that John exists, we are formulating an existential judgment. Man is capable of knowing the existence of things, and so his knowledge has the value of truth. Truth is the agreement of our knowledge with how things are. When we ask whether what someone is saying is true, we want to know whether reality is as he says it is, whether such a state of affairs really exists. If the real development of man depends upon his reaching or desiring real ends, then truth is crucial. The truth prevents us from chasing chimeras, things that are really empty illusions. Fantasy only has meaning when we know it is mere fantasy.

Just as in science truth is contrary to falsehood or error, in the moral sphere truth is contrary to the lie. Error is unintentional, but a lie is intentional. With the exception of jokes, lies are evil from the moral point of view. A lie cannot be justified by any noble purpose. Every man has the right to know the truth, without which his personal life cannot develop. If he is nourished on lies, he loses the ability to distinguish good from evil, and the result is that the hierarchy of goods is permanently upset.

The essence of the lie is most often the desire to use another human person, whether for personal, political or economic ends. Although the freedom of the person who is told the lie is not immediately violated, his will is inclined to what reason presents before it. If reason presents what is false and evil as true and good, it is very likely that the will shall choose that which is evil. We must be very prudent in how we listen to what others are saying. Sometimes we must even know how not to listen.

Lies are disguised as truths, otherwise they would have no purpose. The illusions of truth may be masterfully woven of many truths so that we find it easy to overlook the fundamental lie. We use inductive reasoning spontaneously, and so it is easy to conclude that if most of what someone is saying is true, then it must all be true. This is a very common method of propaganda.

Lies are evil not only for the person who is deceived, but also for the deceiver. The person who utters the lie has something missing inside him. There should be an agreement between what he says and what he knows, but that is lacking. This is a moral evil, because the truth is the foundation of the good of the person. This good is violated by a lie. Speech that is infected with lies strikes directly at the liar, because it violates the established connection between signs and what they mean.

A sign is a sign because it means something. It is not a thing in itself. Signs and their meanings must be linked. When this link is broken, the essence of the sign is destroyed. At the same time, the lie introduces an inner disharmony. The word becomes like a scalpel that kills instead of heals. It kills the truth. It does not matter that the liar himself knows the truth, because the word he speaks is not his private property. Words are the property of the entire human community. They belong to everybody in a way that nothing else does. Since words that are given over to the use of lies destroy man and his entire culture, we must guard this treasure like the apple of our eye. We know this from history. The German people, under the Nazi regime, lived in an atmosphere of lies. The lie was the basic tool in the ideological struggle. The prevalence of lies brought about the worst kind of degradation for its victims. In our own time and culture, we experience the deliberate distortion of words like justice, values, family and even life brought about by social engineers to serve political and economic ends. Truth in advertising is one of those ideals that is all too often violated in our society. Without the truth there is no freedom. Without freedom, man cannot develop.

We must remember that while words are common property, not every truth is common property. There are some things that not everyone has a right to know, such as state and private secrets. Each person has a right to protect his own secrets, and the state has a right to protect its important secrets. When someone asks an inappropriate question, we may either keep silent, or prudently avoid disclosing the truth. This is sometimes easy, but occasionally it requires heroism.

Of all the forms of justice, we must take the greatest care to observe the requirements of commutative justice in our daily life, because we constantly encounter it in our relations with others.

Study and Reflection Questions

1. Does selling goods at a profit violate commutative justice? Why or why not?
2. In what circumstances is charging interest a violation of commutative justice?
3. Explain why man has a right to the truth.
4. How do lies hurt the receiver and the perpetrator of the lie?

Supplemental Readings

Aquinas, Thomas. *Summa Theologiae*, II-II qq. 57-80 (justice in general).

Aquinas, Thomas. *Summa Theologiae*, II-II qq. 109-113 (lying).
Fernández, Aurelio and Socías, James. *A Basic Course on Moral Theology: Our Moral Life in Christ*, pp. 338-339.
Gilson, Etienne. *Moral Values and Moral Life*, pp. 250-268.
Vaske, Martin. *A Philosophy of Morality*, pp. 156-158.

Distributive Justice

Distributive justice concerns the relations of society to the individual. We notice at once that people are not equal with respect to their belongings, accomplishments, or the honors bestowed upon them. Is this inequality acceptable, or does justice require that everyone be forced to the same level? Socialist ideology rejects any form of inequality and proposes that the government should force everyone to the same level. When socialism brings everyone to the same level, it is usually to the lowest level. It is far easier to take property from the rich, to prevent the artist from creating, or to force the scholar to be silent, than to teach the helpless man how to manage his affairs, to teach the less talented how to create, or to teach the lazy student how to study. Equalization leads nowhere. It ends by impoverishing everyone and destroying culture. We must accept the fact that people are different and must remain different.

Justice is not based on equality, but on equity. Equity must consider the different circumstances in which people live, how they work, and how much they contribute to the common good. Distributive justice is exercised first by those who hold power. They are entrusted with caring for the good of the state, and thereby the good of the citizen. They must be very prudent and diligent to distribute various goods to various people according to the right measure.

Some people require special assistance from the state. Some people may require help because of physical or mental weakness. Others are at a disadvantage because they have not acquired any property. For various reasons, some people need the help of the state more than those who are self-sufficient or well situated. Other people who hold positions of high responsibility earn more because they contribute more to the common good. A government minister should earn more than a postal clerk. Although all work is valuable and should be respected if it is performed honestly, the minister has far more responsibility than does the clerk. Where this difference is not respected, the result most often is corruption and dereliction of duty.

The work of the artist and the scholar cannot be measured in terms of immediate profit. They should have the help they need so that they may work without being preoccupied with survival. When they must work directly for money, this adversely affects the quality of their work. We should not forget that all society benefits from the fruits of artistic and scientific work, even if all do not pay for it directly.

We could give many other examples of distributive justice, but these are sufficient to illustrate our point. Ordinary people often have difficulty understanding distributive justice because their point of view is limited by their experience, but those in authority have to move beyond this limitation and think about the welfare of all parts of society. Social life is much more complex than the life of a private individual. The private individual is concerned with commutative justice in his dealings with his fellow citizens and equals. The people responsible for the common good cannot rely on the simple calculations of commutative justice. Distributive justice may be compared to a geometric progression, while commutative justice may be compared to arithmetical equality.

In normal states, all these types of justice are codified in law. In the ideal situation, just action coincides with action in accordance with law. It may happen that the strict observance of the law might cause great injury to some individual, especially if there are heavy penalties. The Romans knew this, and they had an aphorism: *summum ius, summa injuria* — the highest law is the greatest injustice. Law by its nature is general in character and never addresses every concrete circumstance. Legal codes try to deal with this situation, but no matter how many specific clauses legislators add, the result will still be a generalization. The human act, on the other hand, is always performed in a particular context, and it is always affected by the context. The circumstances, such as where, when, with whom, with what ulterior motive, enter into every single act. The singular act can only in part be ordered to such general rules. There are also certain circumstances that we can only examine on an individual basis. What should be our guide in a case where we see that the strict application of the law will result in an injustice? Justice is perfected by fitting judgment, which was called *epikeia* by the Greeks. This virtue of judgment is also called equity, as a supplement to an excessively narrow application of law. In applying the law to difficult circumstances we use our common sense to overstep the general formula and see the concrete instance. In the German legal tradition, the law of the state was the most important value, but in the Latin tradition the appropriateness of the law in a given case was considered because the law itself serves the higher purpose of the good of man. The end of justice is to protect and foster the human good.

Justice is the virtue by which we give to each what is due to him. There are some cases where we have a debt that is impossible to repay. In such cases, it is impossible for us to be just, even though we would want to give others their due. We are not capable of thanking God sufficiently for having created us. Since we cannot return to God what we have received from him, we need religion to express our gratitude. The Polish poet, Jan Kochanowski, wrote: "What do you wish from us, O Lord, in return for your gracious gifts? What kind of beneficence is this, which is beyond all measure?" We cannot thank our parents for having begotten us and raised us. While we cannot give them their just due, we must show them respect and reverence. This kind of respect shown to someone who has given us what can never be repaid was called *pietas* by the Latin poets and philosophers. When we speak of piety today, unfortunately we call to mind a very limited kind of religious practice, but in its original sense, piety was the reverence and gratitude we owe to God, our parents and our country. Piety towards God is expressed in religion. Piety towards our parents is expressed in filial devotion. Piety towards our country is expressed in patriotism. We also owe more than can be repaid to people of great virtue, and the respect and honor we must show toward them was called *observantia* in Latin. We owe this respect to our teachers who opened up the truth before us. The paths of justice are truly difficult, but where justice is realized, "it amazes us more than the rising and setting of the sun," as the Greek poet Euripides wrote.

Study and Reflection Questions

1. How is equity different from equality?
2. How is commutative justice different from distributive justice?
3. Explain how justice demands piety toward God, devotion toward parents and patriotism toward country.

Supplemental Readings

Gilson, Etienne. *Moral Values and Moral Life*, pp. 250-268.
Vaske, Martin. *A Philosophy of Morality*, pp. 156-158.

THE INTERCONNECTION OF THE VIRTUES

Some virtues or skills in science and art stand alone. Someone may have the mental skills to be a good physicist, but the same man will not necessarily be a good chemist. The man who is skilled in mathematics may have no skill in interpreting literary works. The skilled painter does not necessarily possess talent or skill in music. The sculptor is not necessarily a poet. Some people may master several disciplines or arts, but there is no essential connection between one such skill and another. Such people are unusual. They may have a certain multifaceted mental aptitude or exceptional talents. Wilhelm Gottfried Leibniz is an example of a man who mastered many disciplines in science. Leonardo da Vinci is an example of a multifaceted artist.

The moral virtues do not stand alone and apart from one another. A man cannot be prudent if he is cowardly and lacking in self-control. A man cannot be just if he is imprudent. The moral virtues enable us to recognize the fitting good and to seek it. An intelligent person is not a prudent person if he is swayed by fear, a depraved will, or by love of pleasure. Alcibiades is an example of the morally incomplete man. Marcus Junianus Justinus wrote of Alcibiades that quick intelligence was joined with a lack of moral principles, with the result that he was capable of doing anything. Sometimes Alcibiades would apply his extraordinary intelligence for the sake of a great good. Sometimes he would use it to seek a great evil. The Greeks held him at times in high esteem, but on one occasion they banished him. Similarly, a good and upright will does not benefit a man if he does not know how to recognize the fitting good. Prudence, fortitude and justice must be found in the same man, so that he will not attack at the wrong time, and he will not overlook the opportunity to attack because he is too occupied with defending himself. Finally, temperance does not stand alone. It needs the continual help of reason in order to aim at the proper mean. The moral virtues must be integrally connected.

The optimal ensemble of connected virtues was called internal beauty or the beautiful good. The Greek term was *kaloskagothos*. A person acquires this ensemble of virtue and moral beauty only with the passage of much time. He does not acquire it merely by his own efforts, but he needs a proper education, environment and culture. The crowning of the virtues is magnanimity, the possession of a great soul (*magna anima* in Latin). The magnanimous man is able to achieve great and difficult goods.

We have forgotten the virtues today. Our description of the virtues may sound out of touch with reality. However, we should remember that Western civilization over the ages was a human civilization, a civilization that was centered on man. Civilization grew out of the integral education of the human being, which was called *paideia* by the Greeks. Our civilization has gone in a new direction. It is a technical civilization. It is concentrated upon creating instruments and upon consumption. The human good has receded into the background. When we speak of ethics, we must return to the sources of ethics. We must have the good of man in view, not the good of the machine or of business. We must return to the virtues to make our private lives and our environment more human, so that we all may respect the good and be open to the truth.

Study and Reflection Questions

1. What is the beautiful good? How does one acquire it?
2. Why should a person seek to acquire all of the virtues?

Supplemental Readings

Aquinas, Thomas. *Summa Theologiae*, I-II q. 65.
Vaske, Martin. *A Philosophy of Morality*, pp. 152-153.

IS EUDAIMONISM SELFISHNESS?

We may describe classical ethics as eudaimonistic ethics. *Eudaimonia* is a Greek term whose approximate meaning is happiness, and eudaimonistic ethics is the system of ethics based on the natural desire of each person to be happy. This means that classical ethics respects the desire of each and every human person for happiness. The desire for happiness is the motive behind all our actions. Some philosophers, including those who support certain forms of Christian personalism, object that this system of ethics proposes a certain form of selfishness. They say that the correct system of ethics is based on our experience of obligation, our affirmation of the person and our giving of ourselves as a gift to others. We think that these objections come from a basic misunderstanding of eudaimonism.

A selfish person does everything for his own benefit. He loves only himself and if he does something that benefits someone else, it is because he calculates that he will derive some benefit from his action. British empiricism (empiricism being the philosophical doctrine that the only form of knowledge is sense knowledge) proposed selfishness as the self-evident first principle of all human action. In this view we cannot act otherwise than selfishly. Certain British philosophers formed a system of ethics based on selfishness which is called utilitarianism. It has greatly influenced social, political and economic policy in the Western world for more than a century. The utilitarian thinks that the government should seek the greatest happiness for the greatest number, but he also thinks that he can sacrifice the rights of individual persons to achieve this. So under utilitarianism euthanizing the elderly or aborting disabled children would be justifiable to reduce the burden of medical expense on the public. The utilitarian wants to organize society so the selfishness of individuals works for the benefit of all. Let each person act entirely for his own benefit and pleasure and the government will work so others may benefit from it, or so that the selfishness of others may be brought together into a kind of collective selfishness. An example of this is when the government permits or even encourages activities that engender vice because of the revenue that these activities generate for public projects.

Personalism appeared as a counterweight to this position. Personalism condemned all other ethical systems, including classical ethics. Where empiricist ethics boldly promoted selfishness, they thought that classical ethics was also based on the same premise of selfishness, though this was carefully concealed. The slogan of the personalists was love of others as an expression of the first and primary experience of moral obligation. We doubt that personalism really ever addressed the true positions of classical ethics. The desire for happiness cannot be erased from the human heart. However, the desire for happiness is not the same as selfishness. Man has reason and will; he is not blind to the objective good. He can see the objective good of other people.

When we say that the desire for happiness is the natural motor of life, we should understand that this desire is subjective. With the help of the intellect and will, the desire for happiness opens itself to the objective good. I must seek that which is able to satisfy my desire for happiness. When I open my eyes to the good, I am also opening myself to reality. Within reality I see other people who have the same right to happiness as I. This perception connects me with the entire moral order. My objective happiness expands to include more than my private happiness.

I would be wrong to suppose that I respect the moral order

only with a view to my own benefit. I would be forgetting the difference between the end of action and the effect that must accompany it. The end of justice is to render to another what is due to him. By acting in this way, a person becomes just. If a person does not give anything to anyone, he will not be just. Although the person may himself reap benefits from his just act — for instance, he may gain the esteem of others — that does not mean that these benefits were the primary motivation of his just action.

On the other hand, if we face the danger of selfishness at every step, and if the only way to counteract it is to make a completely disinterested gift of ourselves, then we are placing the one who receives our gift in a difficult situation. If the other person receives our gift, he or she receives it as something that benefits him. The receiver receives the gift out of selfishness. The giver has raised himself morally to a higher level, but the cost of his elevation is that the receiver has been lowered in a moral sense. This line of reasoning leads nowhere, except that it may provide a topic for a purely academic argument.

Man's basic problem is to perceive the good and seek it. The virtues are not ends in themselves, but they help man in achieving the good. Skills and habits are necessary in every domain of life. We need virtues in art and science. We go to schools to acquire virtues, and we have mentors and teachers to form us in virtue. The moral domain is like the other domains of life. We need moral skills and habits. Every person needs the moral virtues. Without the virtues, a person will see the good as too difficult. In place of the virtues, he may possess many vices. Perhaps in the end he will produce something good, but only with great effort, as the Latin poet Horace wrote: *Parturiunt montes, nascetur ridiculus mus* — The mountains went into labor, a ridiculous mouse was born.

Study and Reflection Questions

1. What is the basic motive underlying human action in classical ethics? How does this differ from the empiricist and personalist points of view?

Supplemental Readings

Aquinas, Thomas. *Summa Theologiae*, I-II, 1-5.

Aristotle. *Nicomachean Ethics*, bks. 1 & 10.

Fagothey, Austin. *Right and Reason*, pp. 44-85.

Gilson, Etienne. *Moral Values and Moral Life*, pp. 15-51.

Vaske, Martin. *A Philosophy of Morality*, pp. 28-38.

THE THEORY OF NATURAL LAW: DO GOOD!

The domain of human morality is the good. Morality is concerned with the good of the person. When we perceive the good of the person, our perception creates an obligation in our conscience. A decision that is in accord with the conscience is a moral good. A decision that is in discord with the conscience is a moral evil. The connection of man with the good must have a foundation. Man's connection with the good is not governed by the same determinism we see in nature. On the other hand, man does not exist in a moral vacuum where he is the one who decides what is good and evil. We perceive the good, and so good and evil are objective. Our freedom lies in the decision to pursue the good or not to pursue it. Our decision to take a path toward or away from the good is not neutral. As soon as we perceive the good, we also have a moral obligation. Every change we see in nature results from certain internal inclinations. These inclinations are strictly determined. A tree is acting according to the inclinations of its nature when it draws sap, sprouts new leaves, blossoms, bears fruit and generates new trees. The willow and the apple grow in different ways. The growth and life of an animal also exhibit analogous inclinations. If natural beings were not governed by the inclinations of their nature, everything would happen accidentally. We see that accidents are the rare exceptions, and we only perceive them in the context of the stable and orderly changes of nature.

Nature is that which underlies natural changes. The nature of a thing is its essence or form, insofar as this is the basis for change, development and motion. Because nature and natural changes are stable in character, we are able to formulate the laws that are the basis of the natural sciences. If nature were not stable, not only would we see nothing but chaos in the world, but the sciences could not stand. Nature is stable, and because of this our knowledge of the laws of nature becomes more and more precise as we investigate the world.

From the philosophical point of view, the presence of internal inclinations is a sign of teleology. Teleology is the purposeful activity of nature. Nature works for an end. By "end" we do not mean merely the final point of a change, but the internal motive that guides change in a particular direction. If things did not act with an internal motive, change would always be chaotic. If an inclination exists, then its end and purpose can be called a good. Every change leads from something that does not yet exist to something that will exist. It is a passage from potency to act, from what can exist but does not to a certain stage of perfection. Perfection is the realization of something to which an inclination is directed. Perfection is analogous in character. It has more than one meaning. The perfection of a tree is not the same as the perfection of a bird or a horse. The end and good must also be understood in terms of analogy.

As we have seen, each inclination to action is directed toward some good. Goodness and being are interchangeable and so inclinations are aimed at being or existence in some way. We can classify all inclinations in nature according to being. First, all things are inclined to stay in existence. Even a rock has a tendency to remain in existence, its atoms and molecules holding together unless interfered with by some external force. Living things demonstrate even more strongly this tendency for self-preservation. Second, living things have an inclination to transmit existence to others by reproducing. Inanimate objects do not demonstrate this inclination. These two forces of self-preservation and transmission of life are behind all the activities of plants and animals. Man has an additional inclination — the inclination to perfect his existence at a spiritual level. This inclination goes beyond natural inclinations as they are found in other living things and it is part of man's unique existence. The third inclination is rooted in a part of man that does not belong to the realm of nature in the strict sense, but is beyond nature. That part of man causes man to be a person. This part is the immaterial soul that organizes the body and uses the two spiritual powers of intellect and will. While these powers operate above the level of biological nature, there are quasi-natural inclinations in them. We have an inclination to develop our personal life through the truth, the good and the beautiful. The intellect is inclined to know about reality. It is inclined toward the truth. The will is inclined toward the love of the good. The intellect and the will together are inclined toward the beautiful. Our life as persons is realized and perfected when these inclinations achieve their purpose. By the true, the good and the beautiful, man is open to all of reality. He is open to the world of nature and to the world of persons, including his own self. The two basic natural inclinations still operate, but they become an integral part of man's life as a person. The good of life is no longer only natural life, but also the life of the person. Our desire to preserve our life or to transmit life is no longer confined to the purely biological level. By eating, man as a person stays in existence. By the transmission of life, man as a person comes into the world. The end of these inclinations in man is therefore the good of a person.

At the same time, we see that these first inclinations are not realized in a purely determined manner. The inclinations must be filtered through our intellect and will. A man decides what he will eat and when, whether and with whom he will transmit life, how he will seek the truth. The inclinations have a human character, and the way in which they are realized also has a human and personal character.

At this point, the personalized inclinations go on a separate path from nature. We can understand the entire world outside of man in terms of determined laws. Do such laws also govern human life in its dimensions of freedom and rationality? If there are such laws, what is their character? The same kind of laws that govern the lives of plants and animals may also operate in our lives, and perhaps all we can do is to acknowledge them. While this is partially true, there is also something more. While natural things are subject to certain laws without their consent, a man must first understand the laws that concern his life. He recognizes the three fundamental inclinations that are connected with the good of the person. The legal order corresponds to the order of these inclinations. If the end of our action is the good, it is good to the extent that it coincides with these inclinations. The good is not some abstract ideal that we have created for ourselves. It is very concretely joined with our fundamental inclinations. This is the source of the law that governs man, which, since the times of the stoic philosophers, has been called "the natural law." The natural law has two sides or aspects.

The first aspect of the natural law is the law and right to preserve one's life, to transmit life, and to develop as a person. The second aspect is the moral obligation that arises from this right and law. If someone has a right to something, I have an obligation to respect that right. The natural law is at the foundation of morality. It is a law that results from man's nature. When we think of human rights today, we often call to mind such documents as the United Nations' *Declaration of Human Rights*, but we must remember that these rights result from man's nature. They did not come into existence as the result of any decree or treaty. Such decrees may be formal statements of the rights of the human person, but human rights are inviolable in themselves, not as the result of some decree.

The discovery of the natural law is crucial for our understanding of morality and of all positive law. Positive law is law that comes into existence by the decree of the proper authorities. Whenever we make any decision, our conscience is like a compass that shows us whether our decision is in harmony or discord with the natural law. The violation of the rights of another is always a moral evil, whether it is the right to preserve life, to transmit life, or to develop as a person. Positive laws and social customs cannot be the foundation of morality if they violate the natural law. Positive laws that are contrary to the natural law are not true laws at all, and social conventions that flout morality are evil. Such laws and customs do not create any obligation in the conscience. While we see different laws and customs in different societies and historical periods, we cannot infer from this that morality is completely relative, or that convention is the basis of morality.

Morality depends upon the natural law, not upon the positive law. Ancient Egypt and ancient Persia were very advanced civilizations that could boast of their cultural achievements, but these cultural achievements should not blind us to their frequent lapses in morality. The whole machine of civilization, including the laws, customs and religion, was often turned against man. The foundation of culture and civilization is a concern for the good of man, and this is an objective measure of the real achievements of a society.

The three inclinations must be examined together. We must look at them in the light of the most important good, which is the good of the person. When we follow our inclinations, we must use our reason. We cannot follow them blindly. We must eat in a rational manner. We must transmit life in a rational manner. Our search for the truth must be guided by reason. Today, we are still under the influence of the philosophy of Descartes, in which these inclinations have been regarded as separate from the person. This philosophy has had disastrous consequences, and the worst example may be Freudian psychoanalysis. In practice, Freudian psychology recommends that we surrender to nature, especially at the level of the inclination to transmit life. It proclaims full sexual freedom as the norm, that this will liberate man from the yoke of the *superego*. It promises a richer and more pleasurable life as the result. It is a freedom without reason, and it eventually turns against man, making him the slave of his desires. Another moral danger is that sexual license leads to abortion. Freudian psychology has taken over our culture. Sex and force are now raised to the status of gods, but our culture has been brought low. A human being is one unified being. The soul and the body do not exist separately as two beings. Each man is morally responsible for how he uses his inclinations. The path of moral responsibility is not submission to some imaginary *superego*, but the rational approach to the good.

Another danger arises from a lack of respect for the right to the truth, which is connected with the third level of inclination. The truth is threatened in two ways. In totalitarian states, a civilization of lies is forced upon the people. In democratic societies, the truth is threatened by the exaltation of freedom and originality. In the desire to be free and original, intellectuals often forget their responsibility to the truth.

Man is free to seek the truth. When he finds the truth, the truth places restrictions upon him. When he knows and has evidence that something is true, he is no longer free to believe the opposite. He may not disregard the truth in the name of freedom. All have the right to the truth. The truth is a good of the person in the strict sense, even if not all are able to master every truth in every domain. A great responsibility rests upon those who are occupied in learning the truth by virtue of their talents and occupation, such as academic scholars, scientists, and journalists. The results of research are not private property, and the man of truth must consider whether he is acting for the sake of the truth or for his personal glory. On the other hand, we cannot forget that truth is for the sake of man, and science must respect those limits imposed by a concern for the human good. When science moves into areas where it may violate the human good, such as certain aspects of genetic engineering, it becomes something evil.

Our inclinations are integrally connected. In each instance, we must understand the good that is connected with our inclinations. Conversely, if these inclinations are treated as separate, they may become evil. While we have the right to follow our inclinations, this right is limited by the good of the person. Here the analogous nature of the good is most apparent. In certain cases, for example, a man may abstain from food in order to fight for his dignity. A man who chooses to be a priest renounces his right to transmit life. In some religious orders, it was once forbidden to engage in study. In these cases and others, we see that the measure is the relation of our decisions to the good of the person.

The moral order is dynamic. It is connected with our acts of decision. The good is not something toward which we can be neutral. It is inscribed into the dynamism of our life. If this dynamism is not predetermined but requires our consent, then our consent is related to the good by something other than natural necessity. The good of the person does not determine our decisions by virtue of natural necessity, but by virtue of obligation. On the one hand, I do not have to decide on a particular thing. On the other hand, not only may I, but I must pursue the good that is fitting and right. I know this from my experience of conscience.

The only place we encounter obligation is in our human moral life. It is our response to the good we perceive, a good that demands to be realized. The good is always man as a person, who has a natural right to life, to the transmission of life and to his development as a person. He is therefore obliged to act to realize or protect the good. If the life of the person runs its course through that which we have called the good in an analogical sense, the first moral precept that results from the natural law is: "Do good!" We must do good and avoid evil. The other precepts of the natural law are only particular formulations of this first precept.

This is why the virtue of justice and its prudent application in *epikeia* play such an important role in relations between people. Justice is concerned with rendering unto each person what is due to him. That which is due to each person is determined by the natural law. Only if we acknowledge this does our culture become a truly human culture and our civilization a civilization that exists for the sake of man.

Some philosophers of the seventeenth and eighteenth centuries were so concerned with the problem of how to make an inference from what actually is to what should be (in German, from *sein* to *sollen*) that they forgot the order of the natural law as it develops from the three fundamental inclinations. Since they overlooked nature, they had to resort to convention or to *a priori* forms, such as Kant's conception of obligation in which the formal categorical imperative took the place of the real human good. However, I am not morally determined by any *a priori* obligation or precept, but by a concrete and personal good that I perceive.

The conventionalist theory seems to be even more arbitrary.

According to conventionalism, morality is based entirely upon some social contract. Occasionally such a social contract is necessary, such as when we must reach an agreement on the particular ways to organize social life, but it is not the basis of morality. Each man possesses certain inviolable rights because he is a man. These rights do not belong to him simply because some other people agreed to grant him these rights. When social agreements threaten the good of persons, then they are laws in name only and a sign of anarchy.

When someone becomes aware of the principal moral precept, "Do good!", he is not only morally restrained from actions that lead to evil, but he is called to come out of his inertia. At every step, we see that there is much good that we can do. The prospect of achieving good things can give our life a healthy drive and save us from boredom and melancholy. Unfortunately, much of our culture today is dominated by a certain notion of creativity that focuses on the false attraction of evil. The forbidden fruit mentioned in Genesis illustrates this attraction, and the lesson applies today as well. Evil is presented under the guise of good. Evil may be disguised as pseudoscientific theories or as artistic taste. Meanwhile, we should aim at the good and do good. The good is truly attractive. Evil can only be attractive under the guise of good, but in truth it is the lack of good.

In classical metaphysics, the natural law is treated as a reflection of the eternal law. The eternal law is an expression of the plan of creation. The eternal law is realized in man in a unique way. The eternal law is given to man as a task to be done, something that he must interpret and freely bring to realization. Each man has a unique and unrepeatable path of life. He walks his path as he makes decisions for which he is morally responsible before God and his own conscience. Apart from God and ourselves, no one has the right to judge us morally, because no one has access to our conscience. This is the source of man's special dignity, but it also places upon him a great responsibility. He is responsible for the good he should do and for the evil he must avoid. Each man must take his life into his own hands.

Study and Reflection Questions

1. Is good and evil something that a person can define for himself or is it something objective that a person must come to know?

2. Explain how human inclinations are different from animal inclinations or instincts.

3. What is natural law? What is the relationship between natural law, inclinations and the good?

4. Based on information presented in this chapter, what is the basis for the legal rights enshrined in the American constitution?

5. Choose the best answer:

   To understand what is good and evil we should consult:

   a) the laws of the state.

   b) the customs and traditions of our culture.

   c) natural law.

6. True or false: Once we know the natural law and it becomes a part of our conscience any decision we make which is in keeping with our conscience would be morally, subjectively good.

7. Natural law tells us that duties or obligations are the flip side of rights. What do you think society would be like if its citizens only subscribed to their rights and ignored their obligations?

8. Using information from this section and the section on temperance, which of the following describes true freedom?

   a) Following one's natural impulses without restraint — giving free rein to one's impulses.

   b) Using reason to guide natural impulses toward the goods that will bring fulfillment. Using free will to decide how and when to express one's impulses.

Supplemental Readings

Aquinas, Thomas. *Summa Theologiae*, II-II, 90-108.

Gilson, Etienne. *Moral Values and Moral Life*, pp. 193-212.

Krapiec, Mieczyslaw. *Person and Natural Law*.

Maritain, Jacques. *Natural Law: Reflections on Theory & Practice*, pp. 25-38.

Redpath, Peter. *The Moral Wisdom of Saint Thomas: An Introduction*, pp. 121-134.

Vaske, Martin. *A Philosophy of Morality*, pp. 108-119.

5

Conclusion: Morality and Religion

When we discussed the virtue of justice, we briefly mentioned religion as the justice we owe to God. We have emphasized philosophical reasoning as the necessary foundation of ethics. What then is the role of religious beliefs? Is religion important only for simple people who don't fully understand morality, and instead must place all their confidence in religious teachings? We can think of people who follow high moral standards, who are honest and courageous, but who are either indifferent to religion, or who have a religious faith but do not engage in any formal religious observance. On the other hand, many of those who practice their religion seem morally suspect. The morality of those who profess religious belief often provides material for the critics of religion. What is the proper relation of religion and morality? Does an enlightened and upright person need religion, or is religion only for simple and weak people?

I recall an anecdote about a certain Russian woman. After the election of Cardinal Karol Wojtyla as Pope she asked with amazement: "How could this man, who knows so many languages and has written so many books, who even understands philosophy, who is held in such esteem, believe in God?" Of course he believes in God, but the way he believes is far different from what this woman had in mind. The existence of God is not something that we hold on faith, but by reason. Certain precepts of religion are held by faith, such as the belief that God is One and at the same time Three Persons or that God the Father sent His own Son to save us; however, the existence of God is a truth that we can reach without the help of faith. This does not mean that we know the existence of God in the same way that we know the existence of the world or of ourselves. All that we can know of God by reason alone is that it is true that God exists. This truth is necessary. If this were not true, the existence of anything would be irrational, because nothing would have in itself a reason for its own existence. The reason for the existence of things must be a being who has the reason for existence in himself, and this is God. It is interesting that people most often affirm this truth spontaneously. Later they are affected by their cultural environment and a certain kind of education in the sciences. They absorb various views on who God is, how He exists, and how He is related to the world. The result is an array of different opinions, erroneous theories and cults, including agnosticism and atheism.

Atheism, like any negation, presupposes a prior affirmation. We must first know or acknowledge something in order to deny it or reject it. Atheism is not an easy road. It comes from a fervent faith that originates from ideology or philosophy. The motives of the atheist are more often personal than rational. Etienne Gilson, a philosopher of the twentieth century who continued the living heritage of classical philosophy, asked "If God does not exist, why do atheists battle so fiercely against something that does not exist?" The fight against religious practices and beliefs is not atheism in the strict sense, but rather a form of political *Kulturkampf.* It is a cultural struggle. The atheist, since he does not believe in

God, cannot attack God directly, but he directs his attacks against easier targets — the people and institutions of religion.

The attacks of the atheist do not affect only strangers, but also those close to him, even his own family. The Roman historian Marcus Justinus commented on the fratricide committed by the Persian king Cambyses, who is a prototype of the militant atheist. He observed that if a man despises religion and is an enemy to the gods, he can hardly be expected to spare those close to him. This unfortunate truth has also been confirmed by the events of the twentieth century.

We should not forget that some religions occasionally have failed to respect man as a subject. The result has been that man becomes a tool in religious conflicts. Such religious conflicts most often are politically motivated and religion is only a pretext. Due to a misguided faith, many men have been ready to kill and to die at the orders of their leaders. The will of tyrants has been carried out under the guise of the will of God. Instead of being a servant of God, one who freely chooses to act according to God's commandments, a man may become a slave of a tyrant in the name of God. This is false religion and false morality.

The details of particular religious disputes lie outside the scope of this book, but I would like to state that the Catholic religion, as the mainstream of Christianity, has very carefully approached the question of each man's personal moral responsibility for his decisions, no matter what his nationality or religious denomination. Each man is a subject and person capable of understanding and seeking the good. This moral aspect of the Catholic religion is universal. This morality is all the more beautiful when we consider that the most important law in the New Testament is love for one's neighbor, even if that person is an enemy. Neither religious chauvinism nor the kind of tolerance proclaimed today can compete with this command. Tolerance originally meant respect for the right of each man to choose his faith. Today, it has been extended to all spheres of life, including science and law. It has been extended to areas where there is already a rational and verifiable way to show what is true and false, good and evil. As a result, in the name of this new tolerance we become indifferent to evil and falsehood, and if we oppose them, our opposition is regarded as a personal attack upon someone. Tolerance was the proper approach to things that could not be verified, and faith specifically concerns things that cannot be verified by reason and experience. If matters of faith could be verified, there would no longer be faith, but knowledge. The new tolerance, however, is often a deliberate tool of manipulation. In the name of tolerance, we are forced to overlook violations of justice. In the name of tolerance, we treat the common good as if it were personal property. We allow each person to say and do as they wish. A torrent of lies and deception is let loose and we defend it, thinking that we are defending the right to personal convictions. However, if a person's views are his personal goods, why does he need to make them public? If someone makes his views public, they are no longer private, and other people have the right to take a position on them. Others can measure them by objective criteria, not merely as the views of some private person. When we defend lies and deception in the name of a personal right to opinion, we are confusing the private and public order.

The Christian love for one's neighbor is not based only on the fact that each man is a person, but most of all on the fact that each man is a child of God, created in the likeness of God. The transcendental relation of each man to God opens the possibility of a new kind of love, called *caritas* in Latin. In our neighbor, we love a child of God. Each man is a child of God, no matter what his religion, nationality, beliefs or actions. Love is expressed in how we act. It does not remain confined to thought. When our attitude toward others is formed by love as *caritas*, we express it by doing good to them. No man, even if he is a criminal, a thief or a liar, may be excluded from this love, because each one is a child of God. Saint Paul sings the praises of love in his First Epistle to the Corinthians, where he says that love is patient, kind, not envious, not pretentious, not conceited, not prone to anger. Love does not hold grudges. It does not rejoice in evil but rejoices in the truth. Love bears all things and endures forever. This kind of love is beyond the natural ability of nature, and so it needs special help from God. Can there be anything greater than this love that is called *caritas*? Could there be a better foundation for a human civilization? Religious chauvinism cannot provide a better foundation, nor can the tolerance that is at best an expression of indifference toward other people.

What then is the proper relation of religion to morality? Is religion necessary only to ignorant and uneducated people? Let us note first that religion is part of morality as a necessary component of justice. Justice demands that we give to each person what is due to him. We owe more to God than to anyone. We are not able to return to God what we have received from him, because nothing we can do can equal the fact that God has given us existence. Nevertheless we are obligated at least to show our gratitude, and religion is the means of expressing this. Morality requires more from us than a mere theoretical acknowledgment of God's existence. It requires concrete action, just as in any other circumstance where we give someone what is due to them in justice. All the elements of religion — worship, rituals, customs, prayer — are our human ways of paying respect to God. It is morally evil and a violation of justice if they are lacking. It is not enough merely to think about God, our action must be directed to him.

There is another important reason for religion. Man is not completely at home in this world. Our lives are full of doubt, indecision, discomfort, uncertainty and disappointment. Art expresses this in a condensed form. We wonder where we come from and where we are going, but we cannot answer our questions to our satisfaction by reason alone. We do not always have the strength to pursue the fitting good, and the final end and purpose of our life is shrouded in darkness. We know that none of the people and things we love can satisfy our love. None of the things we know, even if we have more and more information, can provide us with knowledge of the first and fundamental reason for our own existence and the existence of the world. We have only an inadequate and indirect knowledge of the ultimate reason for existence. The fact that we formulate these tormenting existential questions shows that the answer to them is most important to us, and that everything else depends upon this answer. Our reason meets a barrier it cannot surmount.

Religion makes the end and purpose of human life clear to us. The end of our life is to be immediately connected with God. God is a person, the infinite Truth, the ultimate Good and supreme Beauty. We may be joined with God by that love called *caritas*, which is a love higher than friendship. It is the beatific vision. Our knowledge of God will be strengthened by grace from God. Our soul will be infinitely full with the vision of God, so that nothing more can be known or loved. Only then will we feel liberated and complete. This is the end and the ultimate happiness of man. All other goods are fleeting and limited, but union with God in the beatific vision is eternal and infinite. By our nature we are open to this good, but imperfectly, and so we need God's help in the form of grace.

Religion is not based on natural knowledge alone, but also on what God has revealed. Revelation completes our rational and natural knowledge. It intensifies our love by showing us the supreme end of love. From the moral point of view this is very important. The central point of morality is the decision, and the decision is based on knowledge. If we see the fitting good in relation to our final end, that is, if we see man in relation to God, we are confirmed in our dignity and no one can rob us of it. Our dignity is no longer based on a code of laws or upon the natural law, but is affirmed by God Himself. There can be no higher affirmation of our dignity. Anything that would undermine this dignity is false.

Could our decisions rest on a better foundation? Revelation is necessary because sometimes culture, ideology and science can be used as weapons against man. They may be misused to reduce man to the status of an animal or a mere part of society. If so, they have become pseudoculture, pseudoideology and pseudoscience. Love as *caritas* also strengthens our attachment to the fitting good so that we are able not only to recognize it, but to pursue it.

A man who has faith is in a better position than the indifferent man or nonbeliever. If a man has faith, the natural virtues may be strengthened supernaturally by grace. Faith is itself a grace, as are hope, love and wisdom. Grace comes from God, and as grace it does not appear as the result of any human merit. A man may share in grace if he prepares himself by prayer and contemplation. His efforts in prayer and contemplation are his contribution, and the grace itself is from God. He may seek these gifts and make his actions stronger with their help. A culture that has no place for prayer and contemplation, but reduces man to the role of a machine or computer operator and which tells him to fill his free time with the passive reception of sensations from the mass media will turn his spiritual life into a sterile desert. It is not surprising that today, when the communications media can bring us news from the other side of the world in seconds, we find it more and more difficult to make contact with our closest neighbors. People may live in adjoining houses, but have very little to say to each other.

The sacraments play an important role in the life of the man who has faith. The sacraments are visible signs whose purpose it is to raise man to that which is spiritual. The sacrament of baptism frees man from original sin. The sacrament of matrimony gives a spiritual dimension to marital love. The sacrament of holy orders gives a man a higher share in the priesthood of Christ. These sacraments and the others (the anointing of the sick, confirmation, confession and holy communion) each have a certain supernatural power that makes it easier for man to approach God.

Along with grace and the sacraments, religion also provides us with examples of how we should act. The decalogue (the ten commandments given through Moses) is a certain development of the natural law and the law revealed by God. Some of the commandments explain the natural law in negative terms. The commandment that says "do not kill" uses negative terms, while the principle in natural law is that every man has a right to life. Some of the commandments are strictly connected with religion, for example, "You shall not have strange gods before me." These commandments address man's weakest points, and on this account they are universal. They are practical for all men. Christ himself has provided concrete examples of how we should live by his life and his teaching. Christ's death on the cross for the salvation of all men is an expression of God's unbounded love for man. We also have examples in the saints and blesseds. Each of the saints possessed some particular virtue to an exceptional degree. As examples, they are not abstract ideals or disembodied values, but real and concrete guides to whom a man of faith may resort in difficult moments.

Religion shows us the end and purpose of our life more clearly. It provides us with help from God in the form of grace, sacraments and the examples of the saints so that we may travel the path that leads to this end. This path that leads to our end is morality. The love of God and the love of our neighbor are the very root of morality. For this reason, the battle against religion is an attack not only upon God, but upon man and upon his inviolable right to happiness through faith, hope and love. The war against religion not only demoralizes individuals, but entire nations and entire generations. We do not have to look far for examples. In the United States the forces of secularism have worked long and hard to remove any trace of God and religion from our schools. The resulting atmosphere of normlessness and indifference has numbed the souls of generations, occasionally manifesting itself in horrific events such as the shootings at Columbine High School.

If men of faith have not always acted rightly, we must leave that as a matter that they must resolve in their own conscience. Every man has his own path. In any case, we do not know whether we would not have acted worse under the same circumstances. A right conscience strengthened by religion is a treasure. It gives us an opportunity to reflect, so that we may recognize our guilt and repent. Christ freed us from the guilt of original sin, but he did not free us from its consequences. The man of faith does not always walk a perfect path. He does not have the patent on the perfect decision and perfect conduct. A right conscience helps in overcoming our inevitable moral failures. On the other hand, if the conscience itself is depraved, it renders us blind to the reality of good and evil and leads us to an inhuman life.

Religion is thus necessary to all people, not only to the simple and the uneducated. The end and purpose of our life remains hidden at the level of natural knowledge, and our natural faculties need a certain supernatural strength which can come to us only through religion. It may seem theoretically possible to separate morality from religion, but in practice this cuts morality off from its roots, because morality grows from love of God and neighbor.

Study and Reflection Questions

1. In what matters is tolerance appropriate? In what matters is tolerance inappropriate?
2. Think of an example of a current situation in our society where tolerance is used to silence criticism of an action or situation which threatens the human good.
3. What does it mean when we say that religion is a necessary component of justice?
4. How is the Christian ideal of *caritas* helpful to a civilization?
5. Describe the ways in which religion helps us lead moral lives (that is, helps us pursue the ultimate good).

Supplemental Readings

Aquinas, Thomas. *Summa Theologiae*, II-II, qq. 81-100.
Ashley, Benedict. *Choosing a World-View and Value-System: An Ecumenical Apologetics*.
Augustine. *Confessions*, Bks. I, IV, VII, VIII, IX.
Fagothey, Austin. *Right and Reason*, pp. 263-274.

Fernández, Aurelio and Socías, James. *A Basic Course on Moral Theology: Our Moral Life in Christ*, pp. 3-47.

Gilson, Etienne. *Moral Values and Moral Life*, pp. 215-232.

Higgins, Thomas. *Man as Man: The Science and Art of Ethics*, pp. 171-190.

John Paul II. *Veritatis Splendor.*

John Paul II. *Fides et Ratio.*

Kreeft, Peter and Tacelli, Ronald. *Handbook of Christian Apologetics*, pp. 29-44.

Maritain, Jacques. *Approaches to God.*

Marshall, Paul and Gilbert, Lela. *Their Blood Cries Out: The World-wide Tragedy of Modern Christians Who are Dying for Their Faith.*

McInerny, Ralph. *A First Glance at Saint Thomas Aquinas,* 9-17.

Lexicon

Abstraction – the mental act whereby we see or take the form or quality of some being from the whole being. It is this process which allows us to see the essence or nature of a being without the matter or even the conditions of matter being present.

Accident – that which exists or inheres in a substance. It is a modification or attribute of a substance. For example, a horse is a substance, but its size, shape, and color are the accidents of the horse.

Act – the perfecting principle of a being; that which makes it to be. (Also see Potency.)

Agnosticism – the belief that there is not enough evidence either to prove or disprove the existence of God.

Appetite – any inclination either toward a suitable object or away from an unsuitable object.

Apprehension – a mental act whereby the intellect seizes the essence of a thing. (See Abstraction.)

Areteology – the study of virtue.

Art – the virtue or habitual right reasoning about things to be made.

Being – that which is, including actual or potential being, within the mind or outside the mind.

Casuistry – the art of resolving problems of conscience. This art fell into ill repute because in many cases it became a way to justify laxity.

Caution - integral part of prudence that seeks to avoid evil especially evil that appears to be good.

Change – the actualization of potency. In an accidental change, the subject remains the same (e.g., Tom gains five pounds); however, in a substantial change, the subject changes and only the prime matter remains the same (e.g., paper burns to ashes).

Chastity – the specific virtue that regulates the sexual appetite according to a person's state in life.

Circumspection – an integral part of prudence; the ability to see what is suitable for the here and now.

Cognition – the process of pursuing either intellectual or sense knowledge.

In this book, cognition generally refers to the pursuit of intellectual knowledge.

Commutative Justice – justice between equals, as between a man and a man or a state and a state. It stresses numerical equality of the exchange between the two parties.

Concept – a nature abstracted by the intellect from an individual being. It is the definition of something. The concept is not what we know first and foremost, but the means by which we first know the object. Hence a concept is what allows us to know what a thing is. The concept is sometimes referred to as species, universal, idea or notion. The process of obtaining a concept is called abstraction (see Abstraction).

Conscience – a judgment of practical reason which applies the knowledge of moral law to each human act.

Contraception – morally speaking, is to intentionally frustrate a primary end of sexual intercourse – procreation. This act is intrinsically evil whether married or not. The use of natural family planning – having marital relations during infertile periods – does not frustrate this primary end of sexual intercourse because the woman is naturally infertile during this time period. God through nature has providentially given the married couple for just reasons a safe, meaningful and a moral way to space the begetting of their children.

Conventionalism – the school of thought that reduces all morality to mere convention or custom of the particular state or culture. This system gives no real reason to be moral.

Courage or Fortitude – the virtue of the irascible appetite that either attacks or endures in danger. Courage is the virtue that strengthens and moderates the irascible appetite when confronted with either pain or danger; it steers the person between the two extremes of cowardice and recklessness.

Culture – for our purpose, it is what develops and refines the human person and includes tastes, manners, social customs and institutions.

Deontological Ethics – an ethical system that reduces morality to duty. It has no direct interest in happiness, God or the God-given inclinations within us.

Determinism – a belief that man lacks the ability to make free decisions, as a result of which there is no moral responsibility in any of our choices. Determinists tend to reduce all reality to matter and generally do not recognize anything immaterial within man. Contrary to this doctrine, our personal experience including our struggle with good and evil seems to indicate that indeed we have free will.

Distributive Justice – the form of justice that exists between society and its members. It entails the proper distribution of benefits and burdens among its members. Distribution is not based on numerical equality (i.e., an equal share) but on proportional equity (i.e., what an individual needs or deserves).

Docility – a key part of prudence which makes a person ready and willing to be taught, as contrasted with stubbornness or close mindedness.

Drunkenness – the inordinate use of intoxicating drink. For the alcoholic, any use of alcohol with the possible exception of medicinal or religious use would be inordinate. Drunkenness is intemperate because it impedes the use of reason and causes further harm to the intoxicated person and those around him or her. In certain cases, a person may become intoxicated under the direct supervision of a competent doctor, for example for the purpose of sedation.

End – the purpose for which an agent exists and acts; correlative with purpose, good and perfection. All creatures have an end or purpose which is their good or perfection.

Essence – refers to what a thing is, its nature.

Eternal Law – the ordinance of divine reason for the entire created universe. This ordinance is built into the very being of creation and hence all creatures receive their purpose through divine reason itself.

Ethics – the science of human conduct as known by natural reason.

Eudaimonism – the theory that man's final end is happiness.

Evil – an absence of a good that ought to be. Evil does not exist *per se*, it is always a negation; for example, if you lose your hand in a car accident, the severed hand is not an evil, the evil is the fact that the hand is severed from the rest of your body.

Faculty – a power within the soul, one of the various capabilities of the soul, e.g., the power of sight or the power of growth. There are at least 18 different faculties or powers within the human soul.

Faith – generally speaking, it is the acceptance of the word of another. When accepting the word of God, it is called Divine faith and is a gift that is infused. An act of Divine faith is the assent of the intellect to Divine truth under the command of the will with the initiation and assistance of grace.

Foresight – an integral part of prudence; the ability to judge the likely future outcomes based on the present contingencies of a situation.

Fortitude – see Courage.

Freedom – in this book, refers to a psychological freedom, i.e., the capacity to choose among options. Freedom presupposes the existence of a soul or immaterial component of the person.

Gluttony – the inordinate use of food and drink. Gluttony among other things dulls the mind and leads to laziness and frivolity.

Golden Mean – simply indicates that virtue is the disposition of choosing between the two extremes of excess and defect. This is determined by reason as filtered through the virtue of prudence. It avoids overshooting or falling short of the mark. So the virtue of courage helps us avoid both rashness and cowardice and temperance is the virtue that keeps us from both overindulgence and insensibility. A word of caution: The mean between two extremes is relative and not absolute. Hence what is temperate for an athlete will not be temperate for an eighty-year-old woman. Generosity will be different for a wealthy man than for a poor beggar. This applies to every virtue. Furthermore, since virtue is the mean one does not apply virtue moderately, but strives to be virtuous always. One is not truthful in moderation; rather truthfulness is the mean between exaggeration and understatement.

Good – all creation knowingly or unknowingly seeks the good. Good is correlative with being because all being is good since it is created by a Divine mind which gives beings their distinct purpose. While all things are good in themselves, morally speaking, good is that which is suitable or befitting for a being.

Habit – a propensity or inclination towards either a good end (virtue) or an evil one (vice).

Hedonism – the theory of ethics that views pleasure as the highest good. While pleasure can be and often is good, hedonism offers no evidence as to why it is the highest good.

Honest Good – the good which we seek that specifically perfects our being. All morally good actions perfect our nature and therefore make us happy. These goods are higher than both pleasant and useful goods.

Immanent – when an agent intrinsically perfects itself (e.g., a plant taking in nutrients to grow) as opposed to a transient action, where a being is perfected by an extrinsic agent acting upon it (e.g., a piece of wood being carved into a statue).

Immaterial – that which has no body or is incorporeal, including the human soul, angels and God. All immaterial beings are by definition incorruptible.

Inclination – see Appetite.

Intentional – refers to the fact that our intellectual ideas present to us the actual things outside the mind and so our knowledge identifies first and foremost with things and not our ideas. Hence there is a union or marriage between the intellect and the thing.

Irascible Appetite – the appetite that propels both animals and humans to resist danger.

Judgment – a mental act whereby the intellect affirms or denies the existence of a subject or of an attribute of a subject. The former expresses our knowledge that something exists (e.g., Bernie exists), while the latter expresses our knowledge of what a thing is (e.g., Bernie is a father, businessman, husband, churchgoer, etc.).

Just War Doctrine – spells out the conditions under which the use of military force is legitimate. These conditions, first pointed out by Saint Augustine, are: (1) authorization by legitimate leaders of the state, (2) just cause, and (3) proper means. One of the developments of the just war doctrine since the time of Saint Augustine is that war must be waged only as a last resort.

Justice – ensuring that each person is given what is due to them.

Law – In the words of Saint Thomas, "Law is an ordinance of reason for the common good promulgated by him who has care of the community." As a result all law should be reasonable, mandatory, authoritative, understandable, and serve the needs of the community.

Legal Justice – the form of justice that describes the obligations of the members to the community; specifically, that each man give to the community what is its due. It is the converse of distributive justice, which is the obligation of the community to its members.

Lust – an inordinate desire for sexual pleasure. Lust has negative consequences upon the lustful person and those people to whom he or she relates. Lusting can lead to sexual addiction and other psychological abnormalities. Lust must be distinguished from these good mental acts: the intellectual appreciation of sexuality as when one encounters an attractive person, the scientific investigation of sexuality as when a doctor checks a woman's breast for lumps, the artistic appreciation of sexuality as is evident in the painting by Pierre Auguste Renoir, *Nude in the Sunlight*, and finally the explicit, but wholesome sexual desire that a married couple has toward each other.

Memory – a key part of prudence. An internal sense or power which allows us to recognize images of past events and place them in their specific temporal context. It is not simply the power to imagine, but the ability to recognize the past as the past.

Metaphysics – the highest of all human sciences. It studies being as being with all of its principles or causes.

Morality – see Ethics.

Moral Relativism – the conviction that there are no moral absolutes.

Natural (Moral) Law – a participation in eternal law whereby man is able to intelligently direct his free actions to their proper end. This law is embedded within the very nature of man.

Philosophy – etymologically, it is the love of wisdom. It is a science that seeks first causes without the direct use of Divine revelation.

Phronesis – practical judgment with regard to practical issues.

Piety – honor or reverence toward those who are responsible for our existence or well-being, including God, parents, country and teachers.

Pleasurable Good – any good that attracts us due to its pleasurableness without consideration of its moral goodness.

Pornography – any medium that morbidly excites the sexual appetite. Pornography must be distinguished from media that portray unclothed humans in a manner that is not calculated to generate sexual excitement. (Also see Lust.)

Positive Law – any legitimate law that is posited or laid down, whether written, oral or gestured.

Potency – the capacity of all beings, particularly material beings, to change. The only being who does not have potency is God.

Prudence – the virtue of knowing how to lead a good life. It is right reason regarding things to be done; whereas art is right reason regarding things to be made.

Rational (Cognitive) Soul – that which makes man to be man and not an animal or a plant. Specifically, it gives man his ability to reason and to choose freely.

Religion – the virtue that inclines man to worship and serve God. Humans consciously or unconsciously have a natural inclination or yearning to connect with a Transcendent Being.

Sensitive Soul – the capacity for sense knowledge. Sensitive souls enable animals to know particulars, like this particular plant or that animal, but not universals, like the definition of a plant or an animal. This ability is evident by their actions. (See Soul.)

Sign – that which leads to a knowledge of something else. It is usually a physical object. For example a red light leads to the knowledge that one must stop here. This is an example of a *conventional sign* because there is no intrinsic connection between a red light and "stop here." In some cultures a red light does not signify "stop here." With *natural signs*, there is an intrinsic connection between the sign and the thing signified. For example, an effect is a natural sign of its cause, or an image of a twenty-six foot oak tree within the brain is the natural sign of the actual twenty-six foot oak tree in the backyard.

Sobriety – consists in the reasonable and temperate use of intoxicating drink. Most adults are physically and emotionally capable of drinking intoxicating drinks in modest quantities and this would constitute sobriety for them. Others are not capable of drinking even a small amount of alcohol for a variety of physical, psychological or other reasons so sobriety for them would be abstinence. (See Drunkenness.)

Society – As Aristotle states in *Politics*, "Man is by nature a political animal." It is natural for man to form societies, but he does so freely and by the prompting of his rational nature. All societies must have (1) two or more members, (2) enduring union, not just a single act, (3) cooperation toward common goals or ends, (4) a bond (pledge, contract or agreement), and (5) authority whereby one or more members can determine the means to the agreed upon goals.

Soul – the first intrinsic principle of life. There are three earthly souls: vegetative, sensitive and rational or human. The higher souls include the powers of the lower souls, but each soul is only one soul. So the sensitive soul includes the vegetative powers and, likewise, the rational soul includes both sensitive and vegetative powers. Moreover, the higher soul always includes the lower powers in its unique way. Therefore in humans, the vegetative and sensitive powers work in a uniquely human manner.

Spiritual – See Immaterial.

Substance – a being that exists in itself unlike an accident which exists in a substance. A cow is a substance whereas its color, which is an accident, exists in the being of the cow.

Superego – it is that part of the Freudian unconscious that closely resembles conscience. It is formed when the child internalizes the values and mores of his parents. However, this Freudian view of conscience overemphasizes social conditioning and neglects the role of reasoning within morality.

Synderesis – refers to the habitual knowledge of general moral principles, for instance, "Do good and avoid evil" or "Treat others as you would like to be treated."

Teleology – the fact that all creation has a purpose or end, and moreover that every action is for the sake of an end. Teleology is important in ethics because it reveals what actions would be good for the human person, i.e., those which help perfect the human person.

Temperance – the virtue of the concupiscible appetite which regulates things like eating, drinking and sex. (See Chastity, Lust, Gluttony, Drunkenness, and Sobriety.)

Transcendental – that which is universally common to all things. All beings have five transcendental properties: something, one, true, good, and beautiful.

Truth – a correct judgment that exists between one's idea of a thing and the actual thing. More technically, it is the adequation of the intellect and the thing.

Useful Good – a good that is desirable only because it will lead to something more desirable. Tools or instruments are useful goods because they help us obtain things that are even more desirable.

Utilitarianism – the theory of ethics, founded by John Stuart Mill and derived from hedonism, in which the morality of something is measured by its usefulness in promoting the overall happiness of the community. Among the drawbacks of utilitarianism is its inability to determine what makes society truly happy.

Vegetative Soul – the lowest form of earthly souls. This kind of soul provides life to plants. Unlike inferior beings such as rocks, plants have intrinsic capacity for growth, nutrition and reproduction.

Vice – a bad habit or inclination.

Virtue – a good habit or inclination.

War – when two or more sovereign states engage in active armed hostility. War can be either just or unjust. (See Just War Doctrine.)

Will – an immaterial rational appetite; it is a faculty or power of the soul which enables one to choose a good known by the intellect. It is attracted toward the good that is proportioned to itself, that is immaterial goods or universals like justice, peace, honesty. It is also attracted to material goods in an immaterial way, as when the person wills a particular in a universal manner. For example, I may choose to eat healthy food *henceforth*, or I may choose *never* to smoke. The will must be distinguished from the sense appetite which is inclined towards concrete material goods in a particular way.

Supplemental Readings

Adler, Mortimer. *Intellect: Mind over Matter*. New York: Macmillan, 1990.

Aertsen, Jan. "The Convertibility of Being and Good in St. Thomas Aquinas." *New Scholasticism* 59 (1985) 449-70.

Aquinas, Thomas. *Selected Writings of St. Thomas Aquinas*. (*The Principles of Nature, On Being and Essence, On the Virtues in General, On Free Choice*) Trans. with introduction and notes by Robert Goodwin. New York: Macmillan Publishing Company, 1965. Numerous other translations and editions.

Aquinas, Thomas. *Summa of the Summa: The Essential Philosophical Passages of St. Thomas Aquinas' Summa Theologica*. Edited and explained for beginners [by] Peter Kreeft. San Francisco, CA: Ignatius Press, 1993. Numerous other translations and editions.

Aristotle. *The Works of Aristotle Translated into English* (12 vols.) Ed. W.D. Ross. Oxford: Clarendon Press, 1921-1952. Numerous other translations and editions.

Ashley, Benedict M. *Choosing a World-View and Value-System: An Ecumenical Apologetics*. New York: Alba House, 2000.

Ashley, Benedict M. *Living the Truth in Love: A Biblical Introduction to Moral Theology*. New York: Alba House, 1996.

Augustine. *The Confessions of Saint Augustine*. Translated by Edward B. Pusey. New York: Collier Books, 1961.

Behe, Michael J. *Darwin's Black Box: The Biochemical Challenge to Evolution*. New York: Simon & Schuster, 1996.

Bonnette, Dennis. *Origin of the Human Species*. Amsterdam and Atlanta, GA: Rodopi, Value Inquiry Book Series, 2001.

Brown, Montague. *The One Minute Philosopher*. Manchester: Sophia Institute Press, 2001.

Cessario, Romanus. *The Moral Virtues and Theological Ethics*. Notre Dame, IN: University of Notre Dame Press, 1991.

Clarke, W. Norris. *Person and Being.* Milwaukee, WI: Marquette University Press, 1993.

Copleston, Frederick Charles. *Aquinas.* Harmondsworth, Middlesex: Penguin Books, 1965.

Dawson, Christopher. *Religion and the Rise of Western Culture.* New York: Image Books, Doubleday, 1958.

DeMarco, Donald. *In My Mother's Womb: The Catholic Church's Defense of Natural Life.* Manassas, VA: Trinity Communications, 1987.

DeMarco, Donald. *The Heart of Virtue: Lessons from Life and Literature Illustrating the Beauty and Value of Moral Character.* San Francisco, CA: Ignatius Press, 1996.

Dennehy, Raymond. *Reason and Dignity.* Washington, DC: University Press of America, 1981.

Fagothey, Austin. *Right and Reason.* 1959. Rockford: Tan Books and Publishers, 2000.

Fernández, Aurelio and Socías, James. *A Basic Course on Moral Theology: Our Moral Life in Christ.* Princeton, NJ: Scepter Publishers, Inc., 1997.

Gilson, Etienne. *The Christian Philosophy of Saint Thomas.* New York: Random House, 1956.

Gilson, Etienne. *Moral Values and Moral Life.* Saint Louis, MO: Herder, 1952.

Higgins, Thomas J. *Man as Man: The Science and Art of Ethics.* 1958. Rockford: Tan Books and Publishers, 1992.

Hildebrand, Dietrich von. *Marriage.* New York: Longmans Green, 1942.

Hildebrand, Dietrich von. *In Defense of Purity.* New York: Sheed & Ward, 1938.

Hittinger, Russell. *A Critique of the New Natural Law Theory.* Notre Dame, IN: University of Notre Dame Press, 1987.

Hudson, Deal and Mancini, Matthew, Ed. *Understanding Maritain: Philosopher and Friend.* Macon, GA: Mercer University Press, 1987.

Hugo, John. *St. Augustine on Nature, Sex, and Marriage.* New York: Scepter Publishers, Inc., 1998.

John Paul II. *Fides et Ratio.* Washington, DC: United States Catholic Conference, 1998.

John Paul II. *Love and Responsibility.* San Francisco, CA: Ignatius Press, 1993.

John Paul II. *On the Family: Apostolic Exhortation (Familiaris Consortio).* Washington, DC: United States Catholic Conference, 1982.

John Paul II. *Veritatis Splendor.* Washington, DC: United States Catholic Conference, 1993.

Krapiec, Mieczyslaw Albert. *Person and Natural Law.* Trans. Maria Szymanska. New York: Peter Lang, 1993.

Kreeft, Peter. *Back to Virtue: Traditional Moral Wisdom for Modern Moral Confusion.* San Francisco, CA: Ignatius Press, 1992.

Kreeft, Peter and Tacelli, Ronald. *Handbook of Christian Apologetics.* Downer's Grove, IL: Intervarsity Press, 1994.

Maritain, Jacques. *An Introduction to the Basic Problems of Moral Philosophy.* Trans. Cornelia N. Borgerhoff. Albany, NY: Magi Books, 1990.

Maritain, Jacques. *An Introduction to Philosophy.* Trans. E.I. Watkin. New York: Sheed & Ward, 1955.

Maritain, Jacques. *Approaches to God.* New York: Harper, 1954.

Maritain, Jacques. *Man and the State.* Chicago, IL: University of Chicago, 1951.

Maritain, Jacques. *Moral Philosophy: An Historical and Critical Survey of the Great Systems.* New York: Scribner, 1964.

Maritain, Jacques. *Natural Law: Reflections on Theory & Practice.* Ed. with intro. and notes by William Sweet. [distributed by University of Chicago Press] South Bend, IN: Saint Augustine's Press, 2001.

Maritain, Jacques. *The Person and the Common Good.* Trans. John Fitzgerald. Notre Dame, IN: University of Notre Dame, 1966.

Marshall, Paul and Gilbert, Lela. *Their Blood Cries Out: The Worldwide Tragedy of Modern Christians who are Dying for their Faith.* Intro. Michael Horowitz. Dallas, TX: Word Publishing, 1997.

May, William. *Moral Absolutes: Catholic Tradition, Current Trends, and the Truth*. Milwaukee, WI: Marquette University Press, 1989.

McInerny, D.Q. *Philosophical Psychology*. Elmhurst, PA: The Alcuin Press, 1999.

McInerny, Ralph. *A First Glance at Saint Thomas Aquinas: A Handbook for Peeping Thomists*. Notre Dame, IN: University of Notre Dame Press, 1990.

McInerny, Ralph. *Saint Thomas Aquinas*. Boston, MA: Twayne Publishers, 1977.

Newman, John Henry. *An Essay in Aid of a Grammar of Assent*. New York: Longmans Green, 1909.

Owens, Josef. *Cognition: An Epistemological Inquiry*. Houston, TX: Center for Thomistic Studies, 1993.

Pieper, Josef. *Fortitude and Temperance*. New York: Pantheon Books, 1954.

Pieper, Josef. *The Four Cardinal Virtues*. Notre Dame, IN: University of Notre Dame Press, 1966.

Pieper, Josef. *Justice*. New York: Pantheon Books, 1955.

Pieper, Josef. *Prudence*. New York: Pantheon Books, 1956.

Pieper, Josef. *Reality and the Good*. Trans. Stella Lange. Chicago, IL: Regnery, 1967.

Pinckaers, Servais. *Morality: The Catholic View*. Trans. Michael Sherwin. South Bend, IN: St. Augustine's Press, 2001.

Plato. *The Dialogues of Plato*. Trans. B. Jowett. Oxford: Oxford University Press, 1892. Numerous other translations and editions.

Pope, Stephen, Ed. *The Ethics of Aquinas*. Washington, DC: Georgetown University Press, 2002.

Ratzinger, Joseph. *Principles of Christian Morality*. Trans. Graham Hamson. San Francisco, CA: Ignatius Press, 1986.

Renard, H. and Vaske, M. *The Philosophy of Man*. (rev. ed.) Milwaukee, WI: The Bruce Publishing Company, 1956.

Redpath, Peter. *The Moral Wisdom of Saint Thomas: An Introduction*. Lanham, NY: University Press of America, 1983.

Ripperger, Chad. *Introduction to the Science of Mental Health*. Lincoln, NE: Fr. Chad Ripperger, 2001.

Simon, Yves. *The Tradition of Natural Law*. New York: Fordham
    University Press, 1965.

Smith, Janet. *Humanae Vitae: A Generation Later*. Washington, DC:
    Catholic University of America Press, 1991.

Sweet, William, Ed. *The Bases of Ethics*. Milwaukee, WI: Marquette
    University Press, 2001.

Torre, Joseph M. de. *Christian Philosophy*. Quezon City, Philippines:
    Vera Reyes, 1980.

Vaske, Martin. *A Philosophy of Morality*. Omaha, NE: Creighton
    University, 1980.

Williams, Thomas, L.C. *Building on Solid Ground: Authentic Values
    and How to Attain Them*. New York: Alba House, 1995.

Woldring, Henk. "Constitutional Democracy in Search of Justification"
    in *Reassessing the Liberal State: Reading Maritain's Man and
    the State*, Ed. Timothy Fuller. Washington DC: Catholic Univer-
    sity of America, 2001, 73-86.

About the Authors:

Piotr Jaroszynski (born 1955) holds the Chair of the Philosophy of Culture at the Catholic University of Lublin, Poland. He works within the framework of classical philosophy. He belongs to the American Catholic Philosophical Association, American Maritain Association and the International Society of Thomas Aquinas. He has written numerous articles and several scholarly books, including *The Controversy Over Beauty* (1992, 2002, in Polish), *Metaphysics and Art* (Peter Lang, 2002), and *Science in Culture* (Rodopi, 2003), as well as many books for a broader public. For his textbook *Ethics: The Drama of the Moral Life* (6th ed., 2002), he received the personal thanks of Pope John Paul II.

Mathew Anderson is assistant professor of philosophy and theology at Ave Maria College of the Americas at San Marcos, Nicaragua and has taught at both Gannon University in Erie, PA and Niagara University near Buffalo, NY. He is currently a doctoral candidate at the Institute for Christian Studies in Toronto, Ontario and the Vrije Universiteit in the Netherlands. He has publications in philosophical psychology, education, ethics and epistemology. He is a member of several philosophical organizations.

ST PAULS

This book was produced by St. Pauls/Alba House, the Society of St. Paul, an international religious congregation of priests and brothers dedicated to serving the Church through the communications media.

For information regarding this and associated ministries of the Pauline Family of Congregations, write to the Vocation Director, Society of St. Paul, P.O. Box 189, 9531 Akron-Canfield Road, Canfield, Ohio 44406-0189. Phone (330) 702-0359; or E-mail: spvocationoffice@aol.com or check our internet site, www.albahouse.org